IDEAL LANDSCAPES
AND THE DEEP MEANING
OF FENG-SHUI

Kongjian Yu

To my parents Shiji Yu and Azhi Shao, who helped me understand the meaning of landscape.

Contents

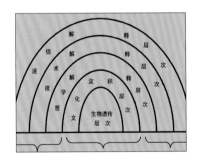

Foreword

After many years of researching Feng-shui and practicing landscape design, Professor Kongjian Yu recently published the important result of his studies: *Ideal Landscapes and The Deep Meaning of Feng-shui: The Patterns of Biological and Cultural Genes.* In fact, the book was completed five years ago, but the publishing was delayed until now.

At the end of 1997, Professor Yu asked me to write the preface for his book, which I was very glad to do. The night I received the manuscript, I started to read it and was soon totally absorbed and found it hard to put down. I read more than half the book that night and finished the rest the next morning. As the manuscript was not too long, I was able to finish it, as it were, in one breath. And after reading it, I felt very content, as if the questions that had puzzled me for years had suddenly been solved by the new perspectives presented in the book. I enjoyed a feeling of enlightenment.

Kongjian Yu and I share similar feelings about Feng-shui. Before the war resisting the Japanese invasion, my grandmother died, and my family invited a Feng-shui master to check our ancestors' graveyard. Suddenly the graveyard became a popular topic, and I learned something about Feng-shui from the family and relatives' chatting. It was full of mystery to me.

During the Japanese invasion, I witnessed the cruelty of the war and the damage it caused to my family. My education and the acquiring of knowledge helped me realize that without science and technology, organization and power, a nation could be bullied, and her people would suffer. Thus a family would not be able to escape disasters. So what was the use of Feng-shui, which could neither protect a home nor save a life? This thought grew stronger after the end of the 1940s. By the 1950s, land reform and communization caused the disappearance of graveyards, and house construction mainly became the business of government and the community. From then on, this backward country, which had been controlled by feudalist thinking for thousands of years, started to wake up and walk the road to modernization. People's lives improved greatly, but no one consulted Feng-shui masters for their choice of graveyard or house. And of course it was not Feng-shui that played a role in the great change in society. At that time, no one talked about Feng-shui.

In the summer of 1983, I went to Canada to study, and in June of that year I was invited to attend the annual conference on geography in Winnipeg. During a group discussion, a Chinese scholar presented a thesis that explored the scientific meaning of Feng-shui. This gave me new inspiration and made me believe that we should summarize Feng-shui scientifically, since it has existed as popular thinking and behavior in China for such a long time.

After coming back from Canada, I became so interested in cultural geography that I started to teach the subject in my department at the university while studying it by myself. I realized that the culture and thinking of human beings are always related to the knowledge and experience gained from life practice in a certain geographic environment. The scientific explanation for the reason that religion appeared helped me understand this. Primitive people relied on some sort of supernatural power as protection and refuge for their fate and souls when they faced the world and life. This was due to a lack of knowledge and to being powerless over their destiny. Supernatural power and its form of reality are the gods, spiritual creatures, and ghosts in religions. Primitive people believed the spiritual world was in control of their fate and their luck, and so should be feared and worshipped.

I believe that Feng-shui is similar to the original religions, which are a continuation of primitive culture. It has simple and reasonable meanings mixed with some nonscientific content, and is often coated with mystery. Therefore, we should look at Feng-shui from the perspective of a process of culture and history, keeping its beneficial content and discarding its useless parts. Since the 1980s, many books have been published analyzing Feng-shui as traditional culture from a scientific and materialistic point of view. These books all reflect how people sought ideal living environments and positions of habitation according to natural conditions such as climate, landform, hydrology, soil quality, and flora, and the combination of all environmental factors. For the same purpose, people extended their search for an ideal living environment to their choice of graveyard for dead family members. Most authors of these Feng-shui books have pointed out that the ideas within Feng-shui such as good or bad luck, fortune for a family, life or death, gain or loss in a business, good or bad results in promotion exams, were really the mystery that people added to it. However, their analysis has lacked a deep exploration of the reason why ideal landscapes were and always are sought after. But Kongjian Yu's work reveals the deep meaning that exists between Feng-shui and ideal landscapes from the patterns of biological and cultural genes. After reading the manuscript, I summarized three characteristics of his work:

1. He believes that the original form of ideal Feng-shui began with primitive people seeking a satisfactory model of habitation.

Professor Yu believes that primitive people came down from the trees in the forest and moved into savannah landscapes that were full of new opportunities and challenges. This forced people to change their habits and look for new food resources and ways to avoid attack from their new adversaries (mainly ferocious animals). Although the most intelligent of all creatures, compared to animals, humans were much less adept at running, jumping, biting, snatching, and carrying weight. In order to survive, they relied on their intellectual prowess, adopting tools and working in teams, taking advantage of the environment to hide themselves when attacking their prey. When the surroundings were not very protective, they would disguise themselves with the things on the ground or climb up trees or rocks to avoid danger. Through trials and failures, people gradually learned about their environment and were able to analyze it and take advantage of it. And they ultimately formed a satisfactory model of habitation—the original model of ideal Feng-shui. Thus Professor Yu's exploration of the original model of ideal Feng-shui begins in the period of primitive hunting, long before agricultural society, where most of the other authors of Feng-shui start their exploration. At the same time, using the example of marmots choosing an appropriate location for caves, the book reveals that animals have inherited an instinct through their genes in the process of choosing and adapting to their environment. As a member of all the creatures of the world, human beings should also possess the gift of choosing a place to live, which is proved by later analysis in the book about the remains of habitations from the Yuanmo primitive people to the cavemen who lived on the tops of mountains.

2. It summarizes the strengthening effect of agriculture in the basin experience in Feng-shui models.

When people's main activity changed from hunting to cultivating, their habitation moved from the mountains and plains to the flood plains, where there was more land to plant. For hunting, people usually used the natural landscape and ground cover as hiding places. By the time they moved into the flood plains, the territory-protecting mindset formed in the age of primitive people was used to deal with other groups of people. Natural landscapes were chosen in which to build cities with "a strong fortress all around" for a nation, and a box-shaped courtyard for a family. In his work, Professor Yu relates property and territory-protecting activity to the typical culture occurring in the special area of the Guanzhong basin in China. And he scientifically explains the developing process of the models of Feng-shui and the relationship between the natural environment and human landscapes.

3. The philosophical thinking and deep meaning of Feng-shui.

After a discussion of the original form of Feng-shui with an emphasis on the models of Feng-shui, Professor Yu's theory reaches the key part, namely, the philosophical thinking and deep meaning of Feng-shui. The author analyzes the basic philosophy of Feng-shui, "Qiism" (the theory that "Qi" is in everything and is everything), which includes three stages: "Huashi" (which means that heaven and earth and everything else in the world began with the Qi of Yin and Yang); "Huaji" (which means that when Qi gathers, it forms signs in heaven and things on earth); and "Huacheng" (which means that to make Qi, both Yin and Yang meet to produce the Qi of life. Once this is gained, blessings and good fortune will come and stay forever). "Feng-shui theory" believes that the Feng-shui of the ancestors' graveyard can decide the fate of their offspring, according to the idea that "Qi works mutually with the senses, and the blessings of the dead are reaching the living." The author points out that this lacks scientific proof. The most important thing is that the author neither enlarges the mysterious sense of Feng-shui by Qiism, in the name of inheriting traditional culture, nor does he "objectively" introduce a philosophical theory, like other authors of Feng-shui books. Instead, he correctly points this out:

"It was not Feng-shui theory that produced the ideal Chinese models (the landscape models). Instead, it was the ideal landscape models in the depth of Chinese people's hearts and culture that brought forth the direct thoughts of Feng-shui theory and further formed a whole set of interpretation systems which were based on Chinese philosophy." At the end of the book, the author concludes, "There is not much meaning in Feng-shui theory itself, but the pursuit of landscape hidden deep within is worth our attention. This is also the starting point of this book."

From the brief introduction above, we can see what makes this book different. It is a book worth reading while Feng-shui theory is popular at the moment. It is concise and written in simple language, with many pictures and illustrations. I believe that the author's research not only explores the deep meaning of Feng-shui, but also reveals and magnifies the essence of traditional Chinese culture in the practice of landscape planning and design, which is the field he works in.

Enyong Wang, Professor at Beijing University

5th of January 1998

Preface

From Plato to Marx, from Aristotle to Confucius, from Jefferson to Sun Yat-sen, human beings have struggled to pursue the dream of an ideal society and have been called by that dream to push for social reform. But quite often, people neglect the dream that accompanies those societal dreams. That is the dream about our environment, which I call ideal landscapes in this book, in order to emphasize the spatial form of the environment.

Ideal landscapes can be explored in various ways. These include the ideal landscapes in fairy tales and religion, for example, the Wonderland,in ancient Chinese fairy tales, the immortal land of blessings in Taoism, and the Western Paradise in Buddhism. There are also the ideal landscapes expressed by artists, in paintings of mountains and water, nature poems, and landscape gardening, as well as the ideal landscapes in daily activities and psychology. The theory of Feng-shui mingles religion, folk beliefs, fairy tales, art, and daily activities together, so it can be comprehensively demonstrated in all of these ideal landscapes. All of the landscape dreams are hidden deep within every person, and every culture, and they often inevitably guide people's landscape designs and transformations. Therefore, discovering human landscape

Figure 1   The landscape of the author's home village Dongyu in Jinhua City, Zhejiang Province where the author spent his childhood from 1963 till 1980, which was much better looking and was unfortunately had been significantly destroyed due to faster development (Photo by the author,1986).

dreams and their deep meaning is just like discovering the dreams we have for society. It is significant for human beings to move out of bondage into freedom, and the creation of a beautiful living environment is especially important. To explore the ideal landscapes in the minds of the Chinese people and in Chinese culture and also to reveal their deep meaning has become the main direction of my research for the last ten years. One of the starting points in this book is to study Feng-shui as a cultural phenomenon and to explore its dream of landscapes and its deep meaning, instead of just analyzing and explaining Feng-shui itself.

Figure 2   *This is the kind of giant Camphor tree in front of the village that the author remember in mind but now cut (Photo by the author, Yantian Village in Wuyuan County, Jianxi Province).*

My Feng-shui experience began when I started to remember things from my childhood. My hometown is a village called Dongyu in Jinhua County, Zhejiang Province. It is located in the Jinqu basin and is surrounded by mountains. The Jinhua River is to the north and Baisha (white sand) stream is to the east of it. In my childhood there was a pine forest in front of the village with a small, clear creek winding its way through the forest and then around in front of my house. Finally, it flowed into many ponds in the village. The ancient camphor trees cast their shade over the white walls and the black tiles. The villagers all believed that they lived on precious land with good Feng-shui. In summer, when dusk fell, the young boys and girls from the village would sit on the black stones at the riverside in front of the gate with the grandmas, uncles, and fathers, and listen to them telling of how their ancestors built the village and set up their homes, and about the experiences of their childhood. Those stories had been told again and again, and many of them were about that dark forest where our ancestors were buried and where their souls were resting and

Figure 3   *The courtyard of the author's home (Photo by the author).*

protecting us. In the evening darkness, every now and then we saw the glistening of a phosphorus fire (they were called ghost fires by the villagers) and heard the cries of owls in the pine forest.

Mystery and fear kept me away from the forest until I was about ten years old. I finally followed my elder brothers into it and was surprised to find it such a beautiful place! Magpies and other birds were nesting in the tall pine trees, some weasels were chasing each other, clear, cool water was running in the creek, and fish were playing among the water plants. After that, the forest became my favorite place, and it still comes into my dreams often like the scene of a forest in a fairy tale. It will stay in my mind forever. Unfortunately, a few years ago, this beautiful Feng-shui forest, together with the Feng-shui tree in front of the village, were sold by some greedy village cadres for only 1,100 yuan (about $150). Now the generations that come after me will not know the awe I felt in my spirit for the Feng-shui forest, and of course they will not be able to experience the fairy-tale-like forest I enjoyed.

I had fear and respect for Feng-shui and its landscapes in my childhood. It was not just because of the mysterious ghost fires and the terrifying owl cries in the Feng-shui forest, but also because I believed it directly affected my fate. Nearly my whole childhood was spent during the Cultural Revolution. Both my parents were the offspring of the "five black categories," and every day after my mother came home from being interrogated and accused, she blamed the bad Feng-shui of the ancestors' graveyard. Later, my elder brother became an anti-revolutionary criminal because he wrote a letter complaining about the Cultural Revolution. And because of this I was rejected many times by primary school and middle school. My mother could not stop complaining about the ancestors' graveyard, and even wanted to have it relocated. Thus I survived my childhood under the shadow of Feng-shui with "bad luck," but it didn't ruin my perception of the beauty of my hometown.

In 1980, I was unexpectedly the only person from my local middle school to pass the university entrance exams, from among over three hundred students.. Praise arrived from all directions, mainly for the good Feng-shui of my ancestors' graveyard and the family house. On the day before I left for Beijing for university life, my mother reminded me to take a spoonful of soil from the Feng-shui forest in front of the village. She wrapped it in a piece of red paper and tied the small parcel with red thread. I cherished it in my suitcase, and from then on this spoonful of soil from my hometown, carrying its wind and water, gods and spirits, accompanied me for many years in the north of China before it followed me across the oceans and traveled around Europe and America. It gave me much comfort.

It seems I had some predestined connection with Feng-shui. I chose landscape architecture (it was called landscape gardening in mainland China at that time) as my major for both bachelor's and master's degrees. In the mid-1980s, when Feng-shui was still a sensitive forbidden topic, I started to question all sorts of relics of "feudal superstition" among the common people, and I visited "Feng-shui masters" in the countryside in order to understand more about Feng-shui. Due to my major and my hobby, I often hiked by myself into the remote countryside with just a water bottle and some bread. I've travelled to many famous mountains and rivers and visited ancient tombs and sacred land over the last ten years. And I've experienced and photographed a variety of landscapes steeped in the legend of mysterious Feng-shui.

As a researcher and practitioner of landscape and urban design, another reason why I'm serious about Feng-shui, a so-called low-class cultural phenomenon, is because of my practical experience in the field. In the early 1990s, a real estate developer invited me to become involved in some landscape planning and design. To my surprise, instead of professional designers, two Feng-shui masters from Hong Kong inspected my design papers. Fortunately, I had respected local Feng-shui beliefs and considered them in my design. It made me realize that a designer should understand and respect the landowner's beliefs in their landscape models. It should be a qualified designer's basic professional and moral standard to respect the local processes of nature and culture, which includes respecting the Feng-shui landscape and its meaning. Of course, I must emphasize here that the designer is to respect and understand the Feng-shui masters' theories and even outstrip them, but not recommend them. And this requires that we designers understand Feng-shui and its meaning in landscape at a higher level.

To get to know the true nature of Feng-shui and its ideal landscape we will discuss the three groups of questions below:

1. What are the structural characteristics of an ideal Feng-shui landscape? What deep meaning do they have?

2. What are the common features between ideal Feng-shui landscapes and other ideal landscapes in Chinese culture? What do these common features show us?

3. What is the difference between Feng-shui and the ideal landscape in Chinese culture and the ideal landscape in other cultures? Why is there a difference?

It is said "traveling ten thousand miles and is like reading ten thousand books." A vast amount of on-the-spot research and experience of landscapes has made me understand more of the deep meaning of Feng-shui. The first thing I experienced was the phenomenon of similar structures between the ideal Feng-shui landscape and other ideal landscapes, especially when I researched some primitive peoples' habitats, such as the remains of the Maba people of Guangdong and the "Xiaonanhai Culture" of Henan. I found that the choice locations of some temples built later were very much the same as the primitive peoples' habitations, and I came to believe that there must exist some kind of biological gene in the ideal landscape models. Further comprehension of this came to me after I studied related works that appeared after the 1970s by Western scholars who acknowledged landscape aesthetics (Kongjian Yu, 1988, 1988a). The works included Appleton's *The Experience of Landscapes* (1975) and his theory of "prospect-refuge," and the environment cognition theory by Kaplan, et al. (1982). These were to a great degree a supplement to the systematic comprehension of landscape aesthetics based on Darwin's theory of human evolution. This helped me to understand the deep meaning of some structures of ideal Feng-shui and landscape from the perspective of human ecology and evolution.

There are many differences between Chinese and Western landscape cultures. Regarding the way of dealing with the axis line, Western ideas emphasize unimpeded views, while Chinese culture pays more attention to the role of the axis in spatial planning. Regarding choices of location, Western culture favors the vantage point and the perspective point, while structures with a hiding and blocking function are more favored in Chinese culture. These differences are hard to understand if we only study them from the point of view of the systematic development of human beings. Therefore, we must investigate ecological experience and the spread of culture. To a certain degree, the theory of geographic environmental determinism has influenced me greatly.

Although many people criticize geographic environmental determinism, I firmly believe that the ecological experience of Chinese culture, especially the ecological experience of the culture-forming period, has played a key role in the formation of our landscape-perception relating to good or bad fortune and the models of ideal landscape. In this book I especially emphasize the significant role of the Guanzhong basin in Shanxi Province in building the landscape dreams of the Chinese people. In order to further prove that the geographic environment and the ecological experience of the culture-forming period played an important role in adapting landscape, I made a special trip to the Mediterranean region to experience and study the landscape under the effect of its unique climate. I paid special attention to Crete and the Greek islands, where European culture originated and formed its patterns. In the areas where European and Chinese cultures were formed, the totally different experiences of ecology and landscape have made me believe that there exists some kind of cultural gene in the models of ideal landscape.

Most of this book was finished in the summer of 1992, when Professor Dingzeng Ai warmly invited me to collaborate with him on a book called *The Quest of Feng-shui*. At that time, I was selling everything I owned (including books) to prepare to study in America. I have to say that were it not for the encouragement and prompting of Professor Ai, I wouldn't have been able to finish the book. The original manuscript became the first chapter of *The Quest of Feng-shui,* which we agreed to publish simultaneously in both mainland China and Taiwan, with the honor of Liyao Cheng, a senior editor of China Building Industry Press, writing the preface for the book in 1993. Later, however, because some of the book's content was related to sensitive issues, it couldn't be published in mainland China. And in Taiwan, the publisher thought the book was overwhelmed by academic theories and lacked commercial value, so it was put to rest for many years. Unexpectedly, Bing Chen from Taiwan Tianyuan publishing house spent a few years tracking me down in order to publish the book. He waited in Beijing until I finished proofreading the last word of the manuscript, and his extreme genuineness and sincerity really touched me.

The core content of the book has been introduced as a research report many times in America, England, Sweden, Greece, and Japan, as well as at Peking University, Tsinghua University, Beijing Forestry University, Shenzhen University, Nanjing Normal University, East China Normal University, the Chinese Academy of Sciences, the Beijing Environmental Association, the Beijing Horticulture Association, and Beijing Urban Planning Institute, in China. There were many genuine feedback suggestions that were a great help in completing this book. Here I want to thank those who made suggestions and also my students. During the process of writing this book, the Laboratory of Systematic Ecology at the Chinese Academy of Sciences, the Fund for Returned Overseas Students at the National Education Ministry, and the National Natural Science Fund (No. 59778010) offered great support with the research work included in the book. I would like to thank Yanlei Zheng and Yongmei Wang for their editing efforts. And finally I want to give thanks to my wife, Qingping Ji, for her support of my work towards this book. She not only freed me from daily housework but also helped with the writing and illustration of the original manuscript.

Kongjian Yu at Peking University
23rd of December, 1997

Introduction:

The history and influence of Feng-shui

Mummy, is Guanyin a man or a woman?" asked the child, staring with puzzled expression at the mysterious statue in Yuantong temple.

"Of course she is a woman," the mother answered, "Look at her beautiful face and fine clothes. It is said she was a princess before she became a nun."

"No, Guanyin is a man and he is truly a brave man!" the father answered and it was not wrong because the Huayan Scripture said so:

"Amitabha, Guanyin is both a man and a woman; and as well is neither a man nor a woman," murmured the buddist abbot, with his hands together and eyes shut.

According to historical records, Feng-shui originated with Huang Shi (at the end of the Qin) dynasty (221–207BC) and beginning of the Han dynasty (202BC–220AD), and was continued by Guo Pu (in the Jin dynasty, 266–420AD) and magnified by Yang Junsong (in the Tang dynasty, 618–907AD). Many books came out later, pretending to be the Feng-shui masters' work (Jiang Guo, the Qing dynasty). In the 1850s, Feng-shui became very popular in mainland China, but was later forbidden for a long period of time. It has always been popular in Taiwan, Hong Kong, and Southeast Asia (Feuchtwang, 1974; Bennett, 1978; Lip, 1979, 1986; Skinner, 1982). Even in some big cities in America, such as New York and Washington, many people believe deeply in Feng-shui. Scholars have different opinions about Feng-shui's popularity, and their opinions are beneficial in clarifying and positioning the points in this book.

From the time of Yates (1868) until now, it has been 150 years since Westerners started to notice and study Feng-shui. But at different times it has been treated differently. Except for a few individuals (such as Johnson, 1881, and Schlegel, 1890), most of the early Christian missionaries and colonists despised Feng-shui as a black art, superstition, or witchcraft (De Groot, 938). Feng-shui was also the greatest impediment to projects in China's modern history, including projects that Westerners considered necessary for the country's development, such as the railways and bridge building (Edkins, 1872; Eitel, 1873; Henry, 1885; Dukes, 1914). According to records, in order to keep similar projects being built continuously, the army had to suppress Feng-shui practitioners' antagonistic activities (Henry, 1885, 150). It was also because of the early Western missionaries and colonists' hatred for Feng-shui that a great number of precious classical works of Feng-shui were destroyed (Needham, 1962).

By the twentieth century, things had changed quite radically. Feng-shui theory attracted more and more Western scholars, its reputation rose considerably, and its role and position in the development of Chinese technology was confirmed by Joseph Lee (Needham, 1956, 1962). Michell (1973) believed that, compared to other Chinese inventions, including gunpowder, typography, and the compass, the Western world had not known or paid enough attention to Feng-shui. This was because the other technologies were easily combined with the Western materialistic value system. Michell declared that the time had come for Western traditional values to change, and for the understanding of Feng-shui to be rebuilt.

Bennett (1978) considered Feng-shui as a kind of astro-ecology and affirmed the philosophy that emphasized the relation between man and the environment in the concept of Feng-shui. He thought that the theory of habitation (Feng-shui) selection was based on the relationship between man and the earth, and even based on the relationship between man and the universe. Lip (1979, 1986) held the same view. They both put Feng-shui in a position comparable with modern ecology and geography. Feng-shui models have even been used in locating archeological sites (Lai, 1974).

Some scholars believe that Feng-shui contributed to traditional Chinese agricultural civilization (Michell, 1973; Skinner, 1982) and have likened it to Chinese acupuncture skills, which have been extensively accepted. The theory of Feng-shui is generally considered to be suitable for both the Eastern and Western worlds (Skinner, 1982; Xu, 1990). Rosspach (1983) thought Feng-shui contained reasonable and logical ingredients as well as unreasonable and illogical things, yet it is a key connection between humans and their environment and between ancient civilization and modern life. This was why some people believed Feng-shui had more advantages than science in dealing with real problems (Feuchtwang, 1978).

We should note that the increased esteem that Western scholars held for Feng-shui developed parallel with their attention to the global environment and ecological crises, from the International Biological Program (IBP) of the 1960s, to Man and Biosphere (MAB) in the 1970s, to the International Geosphere-Biosphere Program (IGBP) of the 1980s. And from the proposal of the concept of the ecosystem to the idea of a total human ecosystem (Naveh and Lieberman, 1984; Naveh, 1991), modern ecologists' ways of dealing with man and nature has come closer to ancient Chinese ways, which are reflected in the theory of Feng-shui, that is, to follow nature. "Design with nature" has been set as the highest standard by modern Western landscape architects (McHarg, 1969), and has become the supporting pillar for important theories of future development in landscape design (Corner, 1992).

When talking about landscapes influenced by Feng-shui, even people who are critical of Feng-shui can't help praising it sometimes. For example, Storrs Turner used to despise Feng-shui but later came to admire it, saying that "Chinese souls must be full of poetry" (quoted from March, 1969). Joseph Lee was full of affection for the Feng-shui landscapes in China and praised them constantly (1956, 361). Anyone who visited the tombs of the thirteen Ming emperors experienced the creativity of the masters of Feng-shui. And Boerschmann (1906–1909) saw the poetic and picturesque beauty of China in its Feng-shui landscapes.

Many scholars have acknowledged Feng-shui's ecological functions, such as the advantages of drainage, maximizing light, and avoiding wind in areas of habitation. A house with good Feng-shui can avoid flood damage while at the same time having the convenience of being near water resources (Freedman, 1966; Lip, 1979; Rossbach, 1983; Knapp, 1986, 1989, 1992).

Psychological and sociological effects have knit Feng-shui into the fabric of Chinese society and people's lives. It is also closely connected with the unity of groups and families, images of individuals, competitions, associations in social and political activities, and the social notions of some groups (Marcel, 1922; Yang, 1970; Freedman, 1966, 1969; Feuchtwang, 1974; Bennett, 1978; Nemech, 1978).

A proven thesis is that the world of "reality" in Chinese eyes is different from the one in the eyes of Westerners (Freedman, 1966; Feuchtwang, 1974). And Feng-shui really is the Chinese people's way of "knowing, sensing and dealing with the real world" (Feuchtwang, 1974, 14). That means, on the one hand, we only get to know and understand Feng-shui from the effects it has on Chinese life—it goes beyond Western values and theory systems. On the other hand, Feng-shui may reflect something in the real world that is beyond Westerners' experience. Therefore, if Feng-shui is combined with some Western models of thinking, it might offer us a method to know the world, and especially our lives, more comprehensively.

I do not intend to discuss the theory and technology of Feng-shui. This should be left to the Feng-shui masters and those scholars who argue endlessly about whether it is real or not. The basic point about Feng-shui in this book is that Feng-shui is a cultural phenomenon that are beyond the judgment based on scientific understanding. Neither despising it as superstition nor promoting it as a science will reveal its true essence. Feng-shui has its deep meaning in human ecology and cultural ecology. This book mainly sets out from the design, structural, or ideal landscape models that are used to explain the environment of Feng-shui, to explore its structural characteristics and deep meaning. We will see that ideal landscape models exist deep within the Chinese people's mind, and that they are built on a pattern of biological and cultural genes. And the "theory" of Feng-shui is a systematic and supplementary explanation for this profound pattern. Knowing the deep meaning of Feng-shui plays a significant role in knowing Chinese people and Chinese culture, in understanding the landscape and its spirit in the Chinese land, and in improving and creating modern landscapes with more meaningful.

The ideal model of Feng-shui

1.1 A model that has been adopted everywhere

Regardless of whether the theory and techniques of Feng-shui are true or not, we know that the main goal of Feng-shui is to select the best locations for houses and graveyards, and that this is so-called good Feng-shui. So how do we get good Feng-shui? Throughout Feng-shui theory, a basic mental model of the entire display is emphasized: "green dragon on the left, white tiger on the right, red bird in front, black tortoise in back." And the ideal staging of this mental model should be "black tortoise dropping its head, red bird dancing, green dragon winding, white tiger squatting" (*The Book of Burial*) (figure 4). Regarding mountains, the ideal landscape that corresponds to this mental model should be as follows: "the building location is on the spot where the hill levels out, with ridges and peaks in the back, a plain (bright hall) in front of it, water flowing gently surrounding the building location, embraced by protective hills on both sides, a view of mountains and welcoming bowing hills in the front" (figure 5).

Figure 4 The mental image model of ideal Feng-shui (illustrated by the author).

An ideal Feng-shui model can be perfectly realized in the process of tomb site selection. One reason for this is that location selection and construction don't have any true utility, no matter how much Feng-shui theory tries to relate the Feng-shui of the tomb to the living person's good or bad fate (more on this later). In addition, the location of a tomb can be selected from within a vast natural environment, so there is a great range to choose from. Therefore, from either a subjective or objective viewpoint, the Feng-shui goal can be achieved in its highest degree. Now let us first study a typical case of ideal Feng-shui in a graveyard.

Figure 5 The landscape model of ideal Feng-shui (traced from ancient Feng-shui records).

Figure 6   The whole view of the Feng-shui landscape of the tombs of thirteen Ming emperors (illustrated by the author).

This ideal model was demonstrated nearly perfectly in the tombs of the thirteen Ming emperors (Kongjian Yu, 1990a, 1990b). It took Jiangxi Feng-shui master Liao Junqing and others more than two years of searching for this location all over Beijing, through mountains and rivers, before it was finalized by the emperor himself, Zhu Di (*A Travel Journal of Mountains and Rivers in Changping*, by Gu Yanwu). Here, the Yan mountain range meanders, embracing the opening space as if an enormous rolling dragon had suddenly stopped and looked backwards. The cemetery leans on Jundu Mountain to the north, while to the south, Dragon Hilland Tiger Hill guard the entrance. Multiple creeks run down from the valley of the surrounding mountains, joining up in the basin (the bright hall). And each tomb faces its own basin and is positioned identically, embraced by mountains and water (figures 6 and 7). The tombs of the Qing emperors have a similarly ideal Feng-shui structure (Jiankui Feng, 1989; Qiheng Wang, 1989).

Figure 7   The Feng-shui landscape of Xian tomb, one of the thirteen tombs of the Ming emperors (photo taken by the author).

The graveyards of common people couldn't be as singular and magnificent as the emperors' cemetery, but when selecting a location, commoners also tried to follow the ideal Feng-shui model as closely as possible. In figures 8 and 9, I record the Feng-shui landscape of the Chen family's ancestral graveyard in Chenghai County, Guangdong Province. This family is well known in China and overseas for being extremely prosperous. According to Feng-shui

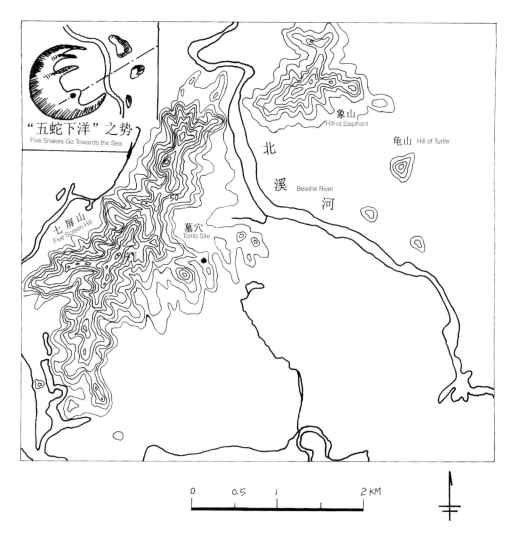

图中文字：
"五蛇下洋"之势
Five Snakes Go Towards the Sea

象山
Hill of Elephant

龟山 Hill of Turtle

北
溪
河 Beixihe River

七屏山
Five Screen Hill

墓穴
Tomb Site

0   0.5   1   2 KM

Figure 8   The diagram of the Feng-shui structure of the Chen family's cemetery in Guangdong; the imposing posture with the imagined force of " five snakes charging into the sea" (illustrated by the author according to research of the place,1:50,000 to the real topography).

theory, this is due to the good Feng-shui of their ancestors' graveyard. Therefore, I think it can be carefully analyzed as a typical case. Most of the tombs face northeast, with Qiping Hill (Seven Screen Hills) in the background and the plain in front. There are hills guarding both sides, and the whole display shows the force of the imposing posture of "five snakes charging into the sea." Tortoise HIll and Elephant Hill are situated in front of the bright hall, locking its entrance,

Figure 9   The entire view of the Chen Family's cemetery in Guangdong (photo taken by the author).

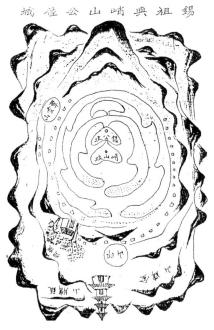

Figure 10 *A typical case of the Feng-shui of an ancestors' graveyard illustrated in a genealogy (from the Genealogy of Huang of Jiangxia)*

Figure 11 *Modifying the structure of the tomb to realize some characteristics of ideal Feng-shui (photo taken by the author).*

Figure 12 *Reforming the direct environment of the tomb to realize some kind of structure of ideal Feng-shui (photo taken by the author).*

while the Beixi River winds its way in front of the bright hall. This sacred landscape is almost the same as in the thirteen Ming tombs mentioned above.

From illustrations and records of ancestors' graveyards belonging to different surname genealogies, we can see similar typical Feng-shui structures (figure 10). The Feng-shui inscription on the tomb of Lai Yuntai (in Bao'an County, Shenzhen), a Qing dynasty general who fought against the minority rebels, describes the ideal Feng-shui for this kind of tomb. The description is helpful in further understanding the characteristics of ideal Feng-shui (figure 13): "It is said that at the bottom of Peng Mountain there was an area called Tiger place, and that was where General Lai Yuntai was buried.… The great mountain originated with boundless force from Centipede Mountain and wound its way down. On top of it, many peaks and ranges pointed to the sky, with lush trees standing tall. At the bottom, there were other mountains where the river stopped, forming a really charming view. It was a place where Yin and Yang joined together. Therefore, when you climb up to the tomb, you see the magnificent secure landscape as if a crouching tiger were guarding the place. So it was called 'thirsty tiger drinking water,' and we knew it was a lucky place by its name." In some circumstances, when it was within their ability, people tried their best to realize some kind of ideal setting of Feng-shui, through the structure of the tomb itself and the improvement of the immediate environment, and also by adding some artificial objects with special significance to the graveyard (figures 11 and 12).

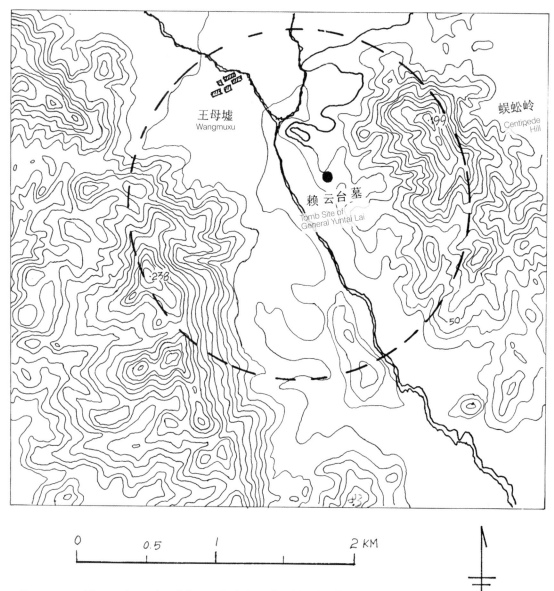

王母墟
Wangmuxu

蜈蚣岭
Centipede
Hill

赖 云 台 墓
Tomb Site of
General Yuntai Lai

0   0.5   2 KM

*Figure 13   The real terrain of Feng-shui described in the Feng-shui inscription
on Yuntai Lai's tomb in Shenzhen (illustrated by the author 1:50,000 to the real
topography).*

Starting with the fundamentals of mountain-land Feng-shui, the theory of Feng-shui extended its ideal model into plain areas with water, calling that Pingyang Feng-shui. This entails judging Feng-shui according to a water system. Both mountain-land Feng-shui and Pingyang Feng-shui are structurally the same, and thus "Pingyang takes the river as a mountain" (*Nine Strategies of Tianyuan*) and "leans on bones [rocks] on the mountains and next to the blood [water] on the plain when burying the deceased" (*Feng-shui Patterns of Burial*). The ideal model of Pingyang Feng-shui is to be embraced by a winding river containing a lively spirit.

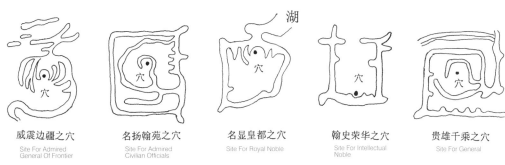

威震边疆之穴
Site For Admired General Of Frontier

名扬翰苑之穴
Site For Admired Civilian Officials

名显皇都之穴
Site For Royal Noble

翰史荣华之穴
Site For Intellectual Noble

贵雄千乘之穴
Site For General

Figure 14   Some typical models of ideal Pingyang Feng-shui (according to Feng-shui patterns of Burial).

Figure 15   The Feng-shui landscape of the emperor Zheng's tomb – a typical case of ideal Pingyang Feng-shui (photo taken by the author).

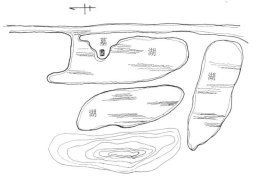

Figure 16   A diagram of the Feng-shui landscape of the remains of emperor Zheng's tomb (illustrated by the author after the research to the actual place).

Figure 17   The Feng-shui landscape of Hong village in the south of Anhui (photo taken by the author)

There are three kinds of relationships between ideal Feng-shui and water; they are described as "riding a dragon" (the water is behind the location of the tomb), "grabbing a dragon" (the water is on the side,) and "climbing a dragon" (with water in front). Of the three styles, "riding a dragon" has the best Feng-shui (according to *Feng-shui Patterns of Burial*). Figure 14 shows a few ideal models of location selection in Pingyang Feng-shui, and we can see they have the same structure and follow the same principal as the mountain-land model.

A typical case of Pingyang Feng-shui is the location of Emperor Daxin Zheng's tomb in the village of Huafu, Chenghai County, in Guangdong Province. Emperor Zheng was one of five emperors in Thailand. He was originally from Huafu, and later emigrated to Thailand with his father, and became emperor. His tomb was built during the Qianlong period of the Qing dynasty, and most of the Feng-shui structure has been well preserved, although the surrounding landscape has changed somewhat. The tomb faces east with a lake at its back, which is the "dragon riding" kind of Feng-shui model. The pattern of the tomb stretches its way

雷岗山
Leigang Hill

宏村
Hongcun Village

意象图
Cognitive Map

0   0.5   1   2 KM

Figure 18   A diagram of the Feng-shui structure of Hong village in the south of Anhui
(illustrated by the author, after research to the place, 1:50,000 to the real topography).

Figure 19   An ideal Feng-shui model of houses (illustrated by the author).

Figure 20   A typical village Feng-shui landscape (Renhua, in Guangdong, photo taken by the author).

into the water and forms a peninsula. Lakes and ponds surround the tomb site on all four sides (figures 15 and 16).

The ideal Feng-shui for houses follows the same principle as that for tombs, the only difference being the size of the setup (*Nine Strategies of Tian Yuan*). Compared with tombs, the location selection and structure of a house are obviously more influenced by practical considerations (such as access conditions or neighborhood relationships). And of course there is less leeway in house design than there is in building a tomb, making it more difficult to achieve ideal Feng-shui. In order to harmonize reality and the Feng-shui dream, some small projects with symbolic meaning, such as a pavilion, bridge,

Figure 21   The designed landform covered with tree grove (Liquidambar formosana) to create a Feng-shui forest functioning as a screen break in front of a village (Batang Village, Huizhou, Anhui Province, Photo by the author).

Figure 22   Temples of earth god or other spirits are integrated with Feng-shui trees (Liquidambar formosana) in front of the village to screen off and safeguard the village (Wuyuan, Jianxi Province, Photo by the author).

Figure 23   Water mouth forest integrated with a pond in front of the village (Xixinan Village, Anhui Province, Photo by the author).

Figure 24   Half moon shaped pond in front of a village with an auspicious Feng-shui meaning (Photo by the author).

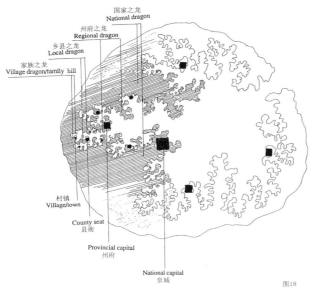

图18

Figure 25   A "segmented" Feng-shui pattern
in China formed by location selection for cities

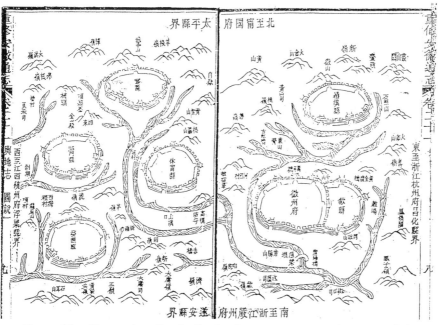

Figure 26   The explanation to the landscape segmented pattern of the
provincial capital county seat in Anhui province (prefecture records of Anhui,
Qing dynasty).

Figure 27   City of Langzhong in Sichuan Province, a city built with ideal Feng-shui,
surrounded with layers of hills and water (Photo by the author).

cellar, pagoda, gate or some natural Feng-shui structures such as a forest and ponds, are usually used to improve the landscape closer to the ideal.

The Feng-shui structure of the village of Hongchunin Yi County in the south of Anhui Province has the general characteristics of village Feng-shui (figures 17 and 18). Researching Chinese folk genealogy can provide abundant information for us to analyze the selection of village locations in planning ideal models. Many authors have done a great deal of work in this area (Xiaoxin He, 1990), so we need not discuss it at length here. The basic model of ideal Feng-shui essentially comprises leaning mountains, surrounding mountains, and a protective screen (figures 19 and 20), and from this basic model we can see the overall characteristics displayed by Chinese villages in basins in mountainous landscape (Yu, 1991).

Many scholars have researched the ideal Feng-shui of urban areas (Heng Qi and Wei Fan, 1989; Jueyuxian'er, 1989; Jingming Lu, 1990; Xixian Yu, 1990). In essence, its pattern is no different from the village Feng-shui model or the model of tombs. Using the same principles and models of Feng-shui from county seats and provincial capitals to the national capital, some kind of "fractal" pattern has been imposed on the whole geography of China (figures 25 and 26).

Figure 28   A Feng-shui landscape of Tiantong Temple (photo taken by the author).

Finally, to understand more about location selection and typical Feng-shui patterns in the structure of temples, we can take a close look at the entire landscape structure of Tiantong Temple (Kongjian Yu, 1991). As with most other Buddhist temples, Tiantong Temple started with monks, and the simple lives they led, inhabiting remote mountains, travelling and preaching Buddhism. The temple initially had no direct connection to Feng-shui theory, but later came to be considered an ideal Feng-shui landscape, receiving high praise from specialists (see Xiaoxin He). Tiantong Temple is located at the foot of Taibai Mountain in the southeast of Ningbo, a city with a sixteen-hundred-year history. It is magnificent in scale and has been designated the second of the top five Buddhist mountains. Japanese Buddhists of the Cao Dongzong school respected Tiantong Temple as the father temple. In an area of about twenty square kilometers, the ridges of the main Taibai mountain range, "winding their way and embracing with passion," form a basin in the middle of the mountains, with its sole entrance (water mouth) in the west connecting the temple with the outside world. Most of the ridges are four hundred to five hundred meters above sea level, and they combine well to form a landscape that stores Qi peacefully. The temple faces south, leaning against Taibai mountain peak like a black tortoise. From both the east and west sides of the main mountain range, two ridges form, meandering gracefully down to the south and protecting the temple on both sides. There are also streams flowing peacefully down from the side hills into the basin (the bright hall) in front of the temple. This combination of rich soil, beautiful water, and thriving vegetation is rarely found in other places. In order to gather more Qi, bamboo and trees were abundantly planted on the protecting side hills, the front of the mountain, and at the water entrance. The track of the stream in front of the temple was redesigned to make it meander and more protective. Ponds with different functions were dug inside and outside the courtyard in order to store water for irrigating the land. A manmade winding pilgrim path and a two-kilometer corridor framed with flourishing pine trees were added along both sides. These artificial landscape features enabled the Feng-shui of the temple to match the ideal model, though it was already a dwelling with all the best attributes of a Feng-shui landscape (figures 28 and 29). The same characteristics can be seen in every temple location on Xishan Mountain in Beijing (figures 30 and 31).

In fact, there are many such examples. If we could avoid some complicated forms and see through all the symbolic Feng-shui signs and attachments that are used for material gain, then the unchanging ideal model that exists in all Feng-shui activities would be revealed to us. And it would work through everything, from the choice of future life environments to the design of modern living spaces; from emperors to common people; from worldly things to divinity; an ideal model is being pursued. In the last thousand years, this model has formed amazing cultural and human landscapes in China (Boerschmann, 1906–1909; Needham, 1980).

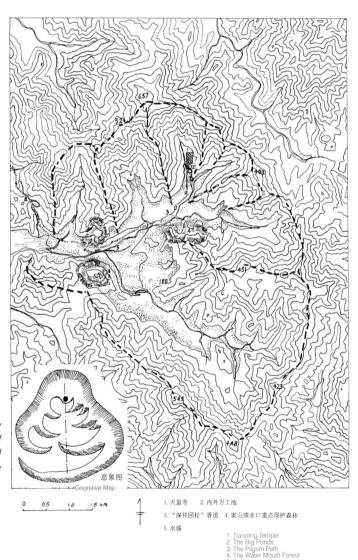

Figure 29 A topography diagram of the Feng-shui of Tiantong Temple (illustrated by the author, 1:50,000 to the realtopography).

意象图
Cognitive Map

0   0.5   1.0   1.5 km

1. 天童寺   2. 内外万工池
3. "深径回松" 香道 4. 案山或水口重点保护森林
5. 水域

1. Tianotng Temple
2. The Big Ponds
3. The Pilgrim Path
4. The Water Mouth Forest
5. Stream

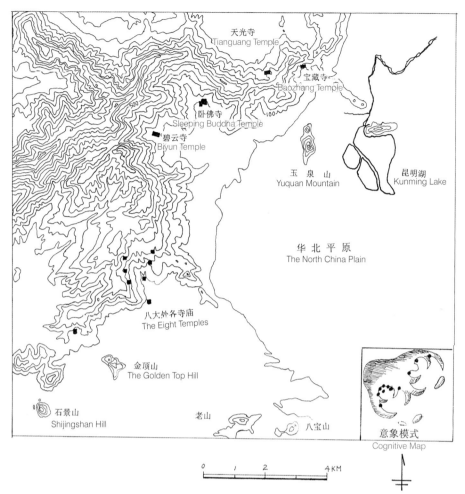

Figure 30   The entire landscape topography of two temples on Xishan Mountain in Beijing (illustrated by the author, 1:50,000 to the real topography).

Figure 31   The entire landscape of Biyun temple (photo taken by the author).

1.2 The basic structure of an ideal Feng-shui model

From the ideal Feng-shui model and a series of typical cases of Feng-shui landscapes mentioned above, we can see two kinds of basic characteristics. One relates to the characteristics of resources—that is, lushly vegetated mountains, beautiful water, rich soil, abundant sunshine, and thriving biodiversity. These characteristics are directly related to material gain and function, so they can be called the practical, ecological element of agriculture.

The other relates to the characteristics of the spatial structure of a landscape, which does not have any practical meaning, and sometimes even has a negative meaning towards the reality of life and material production. But we can get to know the deep meaning of ideal Feng-shui through them. The basic structural characteristics include:

1.2.1 Enclosures and screening

A bright hall with ideal Feng-shui should have "many layers of mountains like fortresses to keep the Qi of the dragon inside it," meaning a landscape of mountain enclosures. Inside the mountain enclosures there are water enclosures: "Big and small streams flow across the bright hall, just like the protecting walls and fortresses of a city, keeping the Qi of the dragon inside … the best characteristic of a water enclosure is to surround and gather" (*Shan Long Lei Yu*, a classic Feng-shui book). In the landscape of mountain and water enclosures, the selected location should be embraced by a protecting hill. There are mountains in the front as screens, and thus a multilayered enclosure is formed with a well-screened space. Except for the natural enclosure and screening, manmade walls, screen walls, and Feng-shui forests surrounding at the strategic locations further serve the function of enclosing and screening.

1.2.2 Close to the edge and with mountain or water support

The ideal location must have a mountain to lean against and be near water. And the best position is at the point where the mountain range levels out. A typical case regards the thirteen Ming tombs. They are located together at one corner of a northern plain, and each of them sits on the edge of the basin where the tombs are located (figure 6–9). Most of the temple locations in Xishan in Beijing have the same features (figures 30 and 31). And the three styles of location selection in Pingyang Feng-shui—the dragon riding, the dragon grabbing, and the dragon climbing, all signify a place that is near or at the edge of water.

1.2.3 Separation and embryo

In an ideal Feng-shui structure, a choice location can be separated and contrasted with the surrounding matrix landscape in the concept of space by selecting a hill out of a mountain, and a high place out of a hill. This forms an independent entity. The choice location either stretches out to become a peninsula or is wrapped by flowing water and stands as an island. There are four kinds of choice locations—Guo (like round-bottomed pot turned up-side down), Chian (In between the legs of a pair of pliers), Ru (breast nipples), and Tu (tip on a high gound). Among them, Tu is considered the best choice. And "an ideal location must be an elevated position ... if not, it cannot be called a real location" (Hanlong Scripture by Guo Jiang). This means that the building location should be high above a bright hall, "just like a cup sitting in a saucer and green grass holding up your feet," looking down at the bright hall and viewing the surrounding mountains. Although the location is leaning on the parent mountain, the pillow mountain

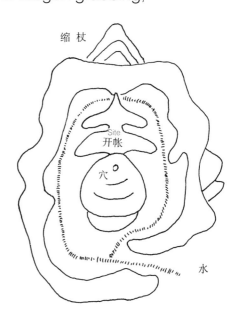

Figure 32   Suozhang and Tai-Si (traced from the ancient book of Feng-shui).

Figure 33   The structural topography of a typical Feng-shui Tai-Si: Anyang in Henan and small southern sea, changed to "Little Nnanhai" (illustrated by author,1:10,000 to the real topography).

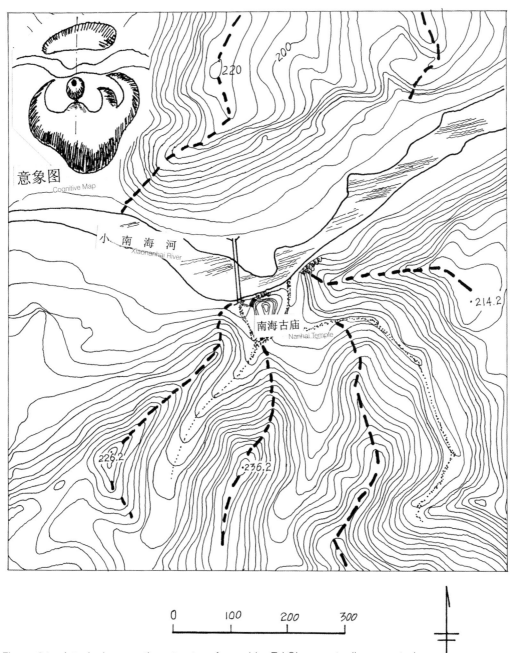

意象图
Cognitive Map

小 南 海 河
Xiaonanhai River

南海古庙
Nanhai Temple

•214.2

226.2

•236.2

0   100   200   300

Figure 34   A typical separating structure formed by Tai-Si—a mutually separated temple location: Anyang in Henan and small southern sea, changed to "Little Nnanhai" (photo taken by the author).

must be "narrow in the middle to clip the Qi inside" and "in the shape of a wasp's waist and crane's knee," which seem broken, but in fact are still joined together. This is the so-called Tai-Xi (life in embryo) of the mountain dragon (figure 32). Tai means that the mountain is born of the parent and ancestor mountains, and Xi means that after the mountain is born, it is separated from the parent mountain and produces another mountain behind it. Thus it forms an ideal location for building. Besides the cases above, the characteristics of separation formed by Tai-Xi are shown more obviously in figures 33 and 34.

In selecting the water dragon, the principle to follow is "the dragon rides the main current, and the building location should be connected with the branches of the water." Big rivers flow fast and roll in waves; they are like male dragons passing by, and will not be able to form Tai-Xi. Big lakes "have spirits of scattering; although they are in the right position, yet they cannot gather Qi. If the outside of the lake is big, but the edge stretches its way into land and forms a small lake, like a bottle neck, or if the current of the outside river runs fast, but on one side the bank curves in slightly, then a delta will appear where the water slows down. Rivers join together here and form a big river and streams. The big river will continue to run away but the small streams will stay in the area and nourish the land. Therefore the land is a noble land because the Tai (embryo) of the dragon is formed here" (Chapter *Jujin* of *Feng-shui Patterns of Burial*). A typical case of what Feng-shui masters call precious land is the Dahao area of Shantou (figures 35 and 36). The vast South China Sea has formed a harbor here, which has become a separate space, with Tortoise Mountain and Snake Mountain locking the entrance.

1.2.4 Entrance and corridor

A bright hall enclosed in a surrounding mountain landscape and a building location surrounded by water are indeed not sealed completely inside. Although many layers of mountain and water keep them within, they do connect with the outside world by a water exit and an airway. The water exit is "the meeting place of the water that flows past the bright hall and the waters that flow down from the dragon and tiger mountains" (*Shan Long Lei Yu*). Generally it can be understood as the entrance or the gate of the surrounding mountain landscape. The taboo for the water exit is that the water surface should not be too wide and spacious or run fast, because it will let the Qi out of the bright hall. The ideal water exit is narrow and winding just like jade chariots guarding the gate. The mountains on both sides of the water exit are called water mouth stars, and the steep, tall peak is called the guarding star. It should close tightly like teeth and stand right next to the water exit. The pairs of mountains that are named—dragon and tiger, lion and elephant, and tortoise

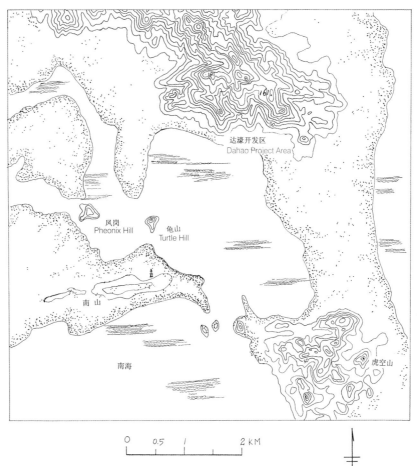

Figure 35   A typical Tai-Si structure; a diagram of the Feng-shui landscape of Dahao developing area in Shantou, which is called noble land (illustrated by the author, 1:50,000 to the real topography).

Figure 36   A typical Tai-Si structure; the entire Feng-shui landscape of Dahao development area (photo taken by the author).

and snake—together form an ideal force of secure guarding. There should also be a guarding star (smaller mountains, etc.) outside the water exit, because "the water exit is like a throat and the guarding star is like a tongue." The building location should also have an entrance, if not it will become like a pond of dead water. Also "the entrance should breathe towards the mountain" (*Shan Long Lei Yu*). Figure 37 shows the consideration of the entrance to the location (the airway) in the author's design of Baoshan Cemetery in Shenzhen. At the left side of the entrance stands a white tiger mountain and at the right side, an azure dragon mountain. Through the entrance of the location, a basin with flourishing vegetation appears with the mountains in the distance greeting it. The view is so wonderful that it is beyond description.

The extension of the entrance in the location is called a corridor. It can actually be a natural valley path or a stream that goes through the mountain landscape and connects the bright hall with the outside world. It can also be artificial or created by strengthening the original natural structure, such as in the divine path of the tombs of the thirteen Ming emperors, which passes through the bright hall connecting the thirteen tombs together. A hidden temple courtyard is often connected to the outside world by a bending corridor with stone stairs (figure 38), and the pilgrim path in the pine trees of Tiantong Temple is a typical manmade corridor (figure 39).

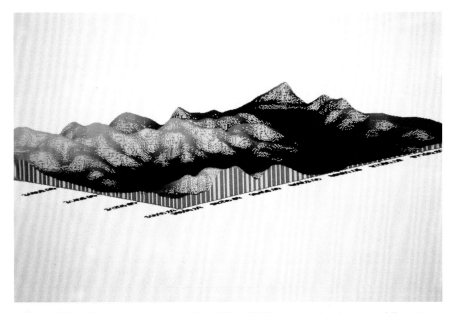

Figure 37   The computer animation of the 3D Feng-shui landscape of Baoshan cemetery in Shenzhen (made by the author).

Figure 38   The long path leading to the hidden temple (photo taken by the author).

Figure 39   The incense path winding through the pine trees of Tiantong temple (photo taken by the author).

1.2.5 Small objects and symbols

In addition to the structural features mentioned above, there are usually small objects in Feng-shui with symbolic meaning (sometimes with some kind of function too) that are used to realize or strengthen some of its ideal characteristics, such as in a pagoda, pavilion, memorial archway, stone sign, reflecting mirror, anti-evil spirit pattern, or gate guardian, for example.

These structural characteristics of an ideal landscape cannot simply be explained in light of practical benefits gained or agricultural ecology, especially when discussing the Feng-shui of tombs. It would be ridiculous to believe that the Qi in the Feng-shui of tombs could affect a living person's life, or that a parent's dead body could gain living Qi and return to life, or that descendants could receive long-lasting blessings because of living Qi (more on this later). Then what is the meaning of the existence of Feng-shui? Where does this model, which has been adopted everywhere, come from? Before answering these questions, let's take a brief look at examples of other kinds of ideal landscapes that took shape separately from Feng-shui, or before it, in order to prove that ideal models of Feng-shui originated from the depths of the Chinese people's hearts with a deeper meaning than we thought.

Figure 40   Small objects and symbols of Feng-shui; Ba Gua map (the eight diagrams) (photo taken by the author).

The same structure with no coincidence

patterns which have originated from the depth of the Chinese people's hearts

2.1 The model of divinity and an immortal land in the Chinese mind

Religious beliefs and myths express not only the dreams that people have for society but also dreams of landscape. We are going to investigate the overall features of an immortal land and divinity in the Chinese mind mainly through both typical and abstract ideal landscape models.

2.1.1 Kunlun Mountain model

Whether in ancient myths or in the legend of Taoism, the Chinese people have always described Kunlun Mountain as the unreachable dreamland of a god mountain and fairyland. The description has been refined again and again until Kunlun Mountain has become an ideal territory where all human desires are satisfied and eternal life is achieved. "Kunlun Mountain is inland in the northwest and is the capital of gods under heaven. Kunlun Mountain covers eight hundred square miles with the height of ten thousand rens" (*Script of Mountains and Seas—Inland West Script*). "At the foot of the mountain, there are nine surrounding rivers with big rolling waves. No one can reach the mountain without a flying vehicle and boat" (*The collection of ancient and modern books, Book of Myths*). Thus we know that Kunlun Mountain is actually a high, steep, lonely island with "nine layers of strong fortresses with the height of eleven thousand miles, one hundred and fourteen steps and two feet, six inches. There are ancient living trees on the mountain with pearl trees, jade trees, trees of life growing in the west, trees of Shatang and Langgan in the east, red trees in the south and green trees and other kinds of jade tree in the north. On the sides there are four hundred and forty gates … the northern gates are open for ventilation. There are all sorts of rooms and activity areas with the garden in the middle of them. The pond in the garden has a branch of the Yellow River running around three times into it and the water is called Danshui (red water), which offers eternal life to anyone who drinks it. There are also He, Chi, Ruo, and Yang, the four rivers running through the garden, which have divine spring water from the highest god. The water can be used to make all sorts of medicines and nourish all lives" (*Book of Huai Nan Zi, Chapter Di Xing Xun*). And in *Heaven Inquiring of*

Songs of Chu the questions were asked: "Where is the foot of Kunlun Mountain? How tall is the fortress city? Who goes through the gates in the four directions? What kind of wind goes through the northwest entrance?" In addition to that, *the Scripture of Mountains and Seas* states: "There are nine gates in the front of Kunlun Mountain with divine beasts guarding them. The divine beasts have the body of a tiger and each of them has nine heads with human faces." And they are guarded by exotic animals and precious birds on all sides. If we do not take into account the complication and disunity of various kinds of exaggerating descriptions, we will see that all these legends of Kunlun Mountain are simply an expression of the characteristics below:

(1) Spatial separation: ten thousand rens high (one ren is about 2.7 meters), isolated by huge rolling waves, attainable only by winged immortals.

(2) Enclosing and screening: nine layers of strong fortresses with God's palace and the immortals' building within, surrounded by rivers and protected by exotic trees.

(3) Gate guards and the entrance: the cities have strong gates that are guarded by divine beasts, while the northern gates are open for ventilation.

(4) Resource characteristics: there are trees, water, and medicine for eternal life as well as all sorts of precious birds and exotic beasts.

2.1.2 Penglai Mountain model

Another model of immortal territory in Chinese myths is "The Immortal Island" in the ocean. Some books say there are three mountains and others say five. The three mountains are Penglai, Fangzhang, and Yingzhou. "It is said the three divine mountains are in the Bohai Sea, not far from land. When disasters struck, lifeboats were blown by the wind, and survivors arrived on the mountains and found the immortals and the remedy for eternal life there. The beasts and birds were all white and the palaces were made of gold and silver" (*The Book of Buddhist Legends*). The "five mountain" theory included Dai Mountain and Yuanqiao Mountain, and Tangwen of *The Book of Lie Zi* says: "Billions of miles away, east of the Bohai Sea, there is a great trench which is actually a valley with no bottom … the mountain is thirty thousand miles high and the flat top is nine thousand miles long. The nearest neighbor is seventy thousand miles away." Usually the divine mountains are called Penglai mountains and therefore we can call them Penglai model. Penglai mountains "face the northeast bank of the Eastern Sea and wind their way for five thousand miles. There is a sea surrounding the mountains called the Black Sea because the water is dark. The waves of the raging sea can reach three hundred Zhang (1 Zhang is roughly equal to 3 meters) when there is no wind blowing, so no one can cross the sea and get to the mountains except the flying immortals" (*Book of Shi ZhouJi*) (figure 41).

As we can see, the divine land of Penglai in the eastern sea, and the immortal territory of Kunlun, inland in the northwest, share some structural

Figure 41   Penglai Mountain model (traced from Sancai Illustrations).

features—high, steep mountains, isolated by rivers and sea, which can only be reached by winged immortals and are rich in pearls, jade, gold, and precious birds and animals. All these demonstrate that the immortal land in the Chinese mind is the result of Chinese people typecasting and modeling ideal landscapes for thousands of years.

2.1.3 The Bottle Gourd model

In the myths and legends of Chinese Taoism, an immortal land should be a bottle gourd, meaning a place with a big cavity a narrow and long corridor. In ancient times, gourds were common containers, and every nationality in China has a legend of someone coming from a bottle gourd (Yaohan Liu, 1985). In Taoism, "Bottle Gourd" means the cavity of the gourd. According to *The Legend of Gods and Immortals* by Hong Ge, there was an immortal called Gourd Man. He hung up a bottle gourd and sold herbal medicine during the day and went inside the gourd to sleep at night. Someone followed him inside one day and found a world of immortals with towers, gates, and paths. The character of the gourd space of the immortals is a narrow passage that leads to a vast space.

The three divine mountains in the sea are also called "three gourds." According to the *Collection of Ancient Legends and Myths*, "the three gourds are the three mountains in the sea. One is called Fang Gourd, which is Fangzhang Mountain; the second is called Peng Gourd, which is Penglai Mountain; the last is called Ying Gourd, which is Yingzhou Mountain. They all have the shape of a bottle gourd." From the illustration of Penglai Mountain in *San Cai Illustrations*, I can briefly trace its shape (figure 41). Therefore, besides the feature of being small at the mouth and big in the cavity, the gourd space also hangs in the air or floats on the surface of water, and this characteristic has certainly added another insuppressible space to it.

Compared to other immortal lands, the territory of the gourd shape, with its small mouth and large cavity, seems more favored by Taoists. So all of the habitations and retreat lands of the immortals are called cavity lands. The well-known thirty-six lands of cavity and seventy-two blessed lands have nearly all taken the model of a gourd space (figures 42 and 43), and their structure has been strengthened by artificial construction (figure 44).

It isn't hard to see that the three models of the immortal land discussed above all have their own individual characteristics. The Kunlun model emphasizes high, steep separation; the Penglai model emphasizes being separated by the sea as an island; and the bottle gourd space model stresses being enclosed and screened by surrounding walls and an entrance that couldn't be any smaller. At the same time, the three models share similar features that reflect the process of idealizing and abstracting the immortal land in the Chinese people's hearts.

Figure 42   An example of a cavity land of blessings; the entire view of Chongxu Temple on Luofu Mountain (photo taken by the author).

Figure 43   An example of a cavity land of blessings; the entire view of Feilai Gorge in Qingyuan (photo taken by the author).

Figure 44 *A strengthened gourd space structure (Qiyun Mountain, photo taken by the author).*

2.2 The ideal landscape model in artists' minds

The degree of idealism in landscapes designed and described by artists matches well with that in the immortal and divine lands. Of course, the God Mountain and immortal territories themselves also contain a great deal of the beautifying works of artists throughout history. Therefore, we need only look at a few typical ideal landscape models that have been deeply influential to discover the basic structural characteristics of ideal landscape models in the minds of Chinese artists.

2.2.1 Tao Yuanming's model

When Tao Yuanming was trying to build the structure of a peaceful, utopian society, he also designed an ideal landscape model: A fisherman sailed along a stream that was bordered on both sides with peach blossoms. At the end of the stream, he saw a cave in the side of a mountain. There seemed to be a light shining inside it. He climbed into the cave and followed a narrow, winding path that widened as it went along, until suddenly a wide opening appeared at the end. There were stretches of field and roads crisscrossing one another. It was another world. When he returned to visit it again, he couldn't find it. This is an extremely idealized model of a basin landscape (figure 47)—a long valley corridor, an entrance that allows only one person to crawl inside like a snake, and a sudden wide cavity at the end. This "corridor + entrance + basin" kind of "land of peach blossoms" has been avidly pursued by generations of artists and scholars, and has struck an extensive responsive chord. It is a recurring theme of Chinese scholars' and artists' work, and has even reappeared in the imperial garden, the Grand View Garden (figure 48). I once used "The Infinit World in a Gourd" as the title of an article to highlight the fact that one of the basic structures of the Chinese classical gardens are gourd-shaped, and that the societal dreams of the garden's owner are built into the ideal landscape of a gourd model (Yu, 1993). The article garnered a long-lasting positive response that reflects a dream in Chinese culture for the lifestyle of hiding in a place and enjoying a peaceful life, as well as pursuing a perfect society. It also vividly reflects that Chinese culture strongly favors this landscape model of "a gourd with a stock" (corridor + cavity).

Figure 45   A real Landscape of Peach Blossom landscape with a legendary entrancing cave at the end of a stream corridor (Bamei in Yunnan Province, Photo by the author).

Figure 46   A minority ethnic village occupied the remote basin for hundreds of years and now become a tourist attraction because of its similarity to the Land of Peach blossoms (Bamei in Yunnan Province, Photo by the author).

Figure 47   A mountain basin which is close to the model of "The Land of Peach Blossoms" (Guangxi, photo taken by the author)

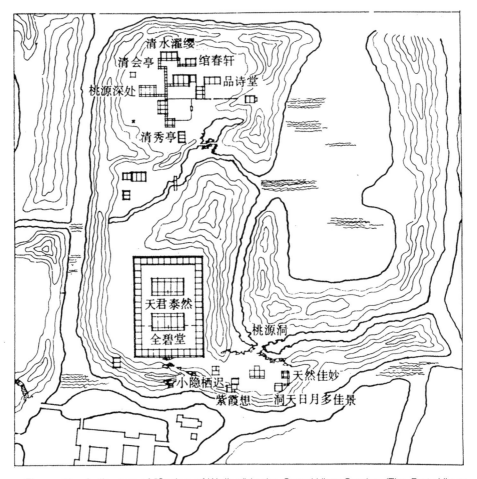

Figure 48   A diagram of "Spring of Wuling" in the Grand View Garden (The Forty Views of the Grand Garden of Yuanmingyuan).

2.2.2 Dwellings in the mountains—the ideal model in Chinese landscape paintings

Chinese landscape painting emphasizes the charm of the spirit and believes that skills are learned from teachers, but inspiration comes from the heart. "There are six principles in Chinese landscape painting. One is to create a vivid charm of the spirit, which cannot be learned, but is something one is born with that is taught by nature. But you can still learn something after reading ten thousand books and traveling ten thousand miles. By then, your heart will be freed from worldly dust, and naturally the mountains will be built in your mind so that when you paint, the charm of the mountains and water will appear on paper" (discussion of painting in The Painting Room by Dong Qichang). Depicting places for welling in the mountains is considered to be one of the major characteristics of Chinese landscape painting (Lifu Wu, 1983). The ancient landscape painters used their hearts to receive nature and used nature to express their hearts. And on small pieces of paper, they expressed their dreams. In those masterpieces of natural landscape painting, we can see the reflections of the landscape dreams of Chinese artists who were thought "to be born with and to be taught by nature." This kind of dream is in a sense a dream of habitations: "some landscapes are for us to walk around in, some are for watching, traveling in, or some for dwelling in… but the first two kinds of landscape are not as good as the last two kinds. Why? Look at the mountains and water today, they cover a few hundred square kilometers of land, but among ten of them, we can hardly find three or four landscapes in which to live or travel. Men of noble character are those who love and desire forests and springs, and that is why those landscapes are called good places. Therefore, painters should take this as the theme for their works, and people who appreciate their works should understand them by the same theme" (Songs of Forests and Springs, by Xi Guo and Si Guo). Whether we are painting or appreciating a painting, it is virtually a process of selecting locations for dwelling.

During the Dongjin dynasty (317–420AD), Gu Kaizhi distinguished the art of Chinese natural landscape painting from being merely the background of a painting. From there, it developed as an individual art in the Tang dynasty (618–907AD), and matured in skills and structure in the Wudai (907–960AD)and Song (960–1279AD) dynasties. This laid the foundation for the later development of landscape painting and completed a great change in the history of Chinese landscape painting (Tianshou Pan, 1983). Among the artists in this period of change, Jing Hao, Guan Gong, Dong, Yuan and Ju Ran had the most influence. "The commentators said that Jing and Guan, followed by Dong and Ju set the six principles for landscape painting, and they were the people who enlightened the later artists" (Wuchang Zheng, 1985). Therefore, when we look at representative works of these masters of generations, we find an ideal landscape model that is in harmony with human desire and lacks artificiality. And these works were copied and traced by people for generations. This in itself shows that the ideal landscape (the dwelling place) that the masters expressed resonated extensively. Jing Hao, who was recognized as the pioneer among those masters, was famous between the Tang dynasty and the whole reforming and interim period of the Wudai dynasty and played a role in linking the past with the future.

Jing Hao, who lived in Hennan Province and retreated into Hong Valley at Linlu Hill in the southern Taihang Mountains, called himself "Man of Hong Valley." Huge mountains, big trees, and an panoramic view are the main features of his water-ink paintings. From the structure of the paintings, we can see the ideal characteristics of the dwelling place or potential dwelling place that he preferred (figure 49). In analyzing the typical landscape of Linlu Mountain, where Jing Hao retreated to, we can further understand the features of the Jing Hao model. The attached figure in this page depicted a typical gorge landscape around Linlu Hill in the southern Taihang Mountains. Due to river erosion, a series of surrounding valleys were formed along both sides of the valley, resembling a cluster of peaks (Yu, 1991 a, b). The differences in lithology caused the rocks to form many stairlike platforms in the surrounding valley. And on each platform there were dwellings that all faced the deep gully, leaned on the cliff at the back, and were surrounded by steep hills in all directions. There was only a narrow pass connecting the upper and lower platforms, and the differences in lithology between the rock-formed caves which could be dwelling places was the same as that in the deep cloudy mountains. They were high above cliffs and steep rocks with spatial separation, hiding in a dark place, but still with a full view of green mountains screening in the front.

Cognitive Map

Figure 49 Hao Jing model; an analysis of the entire structure of Kuanghu painting (analysed by the author).

Figure 50   The typical gorge landscape of Linlu Mountain; surrounding valley (photo taken by the author).

In short, in the gorge landscape of the southern Taihang Mountains mentioned above, there are dwellings "in the painting" (the mountain cottages in the valley and on each step of the eroded platform), or potential dwellings (cliff rocks or caves). Leaning on the steep mountains, they are surrounded by cliffs and steep rock, shaded by thick, thriving forest and only accessible through a narrow rocky path or a creek in the valley. These typical landscape features reappeared perfectly in the Kuanglu Tu painting by Jing Hao. Both the artist's choice of dwelling locations and the "dwelling in the mountain and valley" in his artwork resonated with those who appreciated his work, which has been traced by many generations of artists. There seems to be an internal acting force that is none other than the dream of landscape in the depths of the Chinese people's hearts.

Guan Gong imitated Jing Hao, and their works are structurally similar. Whether this similarity is due to their relationship as teacher and student, or because of a kind of creativity that happened without prior consultation, "gained from the imaginations within the heart," it reflected both artists' common dream and pursuit. The landscapes in Master Guan's paintings look like this: "tightly closed on four sides so that no human foot can get through; among the steep rocky hills, there is a mansion with cranes and surrounding flowers and bamboo. There are people roaming around with staffs and shoes. They are all in feather clothes, arriving with the breeze. If it is not a dwelling of the immortals, then what is it?" (Art Works of Deyu Room, by Li Fangshu). Here we seem to once again see the immortal land model mentioned above. Later, Guan and Jing's painting style was imitated by Fan Kuan, Cheng, and Guo Xi of the Northern Song Dynasty (960–1127AD), and was developed into one of the most influential styles during and after the Northern Song Dynasty. Although painting skills have developed and changed, we still notice a kind of familiar, basic pattern in the structure of the paintings (figures 51 and 52). And later still, comments on the work of Guo Xi, which proposed livable landscape as the highest standard, revealed the basic features of the design: "giant barriers and steep hills, old and tall pine trees, winding creek and sudden cliff, with rocky ridges and peaks rising and falling gracefully" (A Collection of Paintings and Calligraphy of Peiwen Room, see Shouming Wu, 1988).

Cognitive Map

Figure 51 The structure
of Kuan Fan's Painting of
Travelling in the Mountai of
Streams (analyzed by the
author).

Cognitive Map

Figure 52   The structure of Xi Guo's Painting of Early Spring (analyzed by the author).

The "Jing and Guan" painting faction discussed above represents the painting style of northern China, while the "Dong and Ju" painting faction is considered to be the correct transmission of landscape painting in the south. Both factions exerted a similar influence on Chinese landscape painting, and most of the famous artists of the Song, Yuan (1271–1368AD), Ming (1368–1644AD), and Qing (1636–1912AD) dynasties imitated their skills. "By the period of the Ming and Qing dynasties, there was no one among the landscape painters who did not sing high praises of Dong and Ju." Investigating their representative works, we discover the mental model behind the dwelling in the mountains designed by the two great masters. Also, we can see the inner structure in those works that resonated so strongly among later Chinese artists. Figure 53 is Dong Yuan's representative work, The Painting of Xiaoxiang. It shows a vast surface of water, with one peninsula covered by forest and grass, stretching its way into the water. Another peninsula surrounds the other side of the water, with its curve forming a small inlet. Here the water surface makes up a spatial barrier, and a tiny ferry introduces a link between the vast water and the small inlet without changing the sense of separation (in some sense it functions as an entrance and corridor). The living place is a kind of biological transition area (the edging area), which brings out the characteristics of leaning on the mountain (and the river) and being close to the edge. In the representative work of Ju Ran (figure 54), all these features of a dwelling place, such as enclosing and screening, spatial separation, being close to the edge, entrance and corridor,

Figure 53   The structure of Yuan Dong's Painting of Xiaoxiang (analyzed by the author).

Cognitive Map

Figure 54   The structure of Ju Ran's Painting of Seeking the way in Autumn Mountain (analyzed by the author).

are manifested more obviously. We have already seen that although the northern and southern factions of painting have great differences in manifesting skills and choosing landscape objects, the essence of the basic structuring pattern in their works of "setting up a dwelling on the mountains" (the structure of livable landscape) comes from the same "bloodline."

If we think that ideal landscape in Tao Yuanming's model was merely a stage in a peaceful, ideal society, then in the "Jing and Guan" and "Dong and Ju" landscape painting models and in the structure of "building a dwelling place in the landscape," we can see that landscape artists have completely eradicated society and are immersed in nature. The man with the staff and the fisherman represent "me" and the shelters in the landscape (which include valleys, caves, cliffs, and platforms, etc.) are "my" dwelling places. From these models, we can even see that the artists almost shake off any of the utilitarian functions of landscape. All of the landscape features in The Land of Peach Blossoms that would have commercial functions in real life, such as a fertile field, productive pond, bamboo grove, crossing roads, dogs and chickens, etc., are neglected, but through structuring the landscape, an ideal world of "born to know it" and "taught by nature" and "worldly dust shaken off," which comes from the heart, is expressed clearly. Therefore, landscape paintings also become a kind of "artificial nature" and the expression of a human being's soul. This is the unique aesthetic standard of Chinese landscape painting (Daojian Pi, 1982). In this sense, the structure of livable landscape in Chinese landscape painting should contain most of the ideal characteristics. Taking this as a mirror, we may further know the ideal features of landscape in the models mentioned above.

2.3 The ideal landscape model of statistical psychology

Using statistics to measure people's taste for landscape is a more direct and effective way of exploring and analyzing an ideal landscape model. My research over the past years shows this: Among Chinese people with a mid-level education (high school) and above from different backgrounds, there is a general common aesthetic preference (Kongjian Yu, 1988, 1990, 1992a; Kongjian Yu, Qingping Ji, 1991; Yu, 1994). There is an obvious difference between urban citizens with a mid-level education and above and people living in the countryside with very little education. And the difference is mainly reflected in the aesthetic attitude towards some specific kinds of landscape types. For example, the rural folks' aesthetic preference in modern tourism facilities and agricultural landscape is obviously higher than that of the urban group. But no differences are found in preferences regarding the spatial structure of landscapebetween the two groups of people. The difference between the two groups is considered to be due to the country folks' interest in the utilitarian functions of landscape and the intellectuals' aesthetic preference in landscape having more of a tendency to pursue perfection in beauty rather than functionality and utility (Kongjian Yu, 1992; Yu, 1994). An interest in commercial functions can cover up people's genuine aesthetic attitudes (Hull and Revell, 1989).

Based on this, we can say that to a large degree, Chinese university students' ideal landscape models reflect the ideal model of the Chinese people and Chinese culture in general. The table below shows the result of a psychological survey of 87 university students (Yu, 1990). The survey allowed a free style, asking students to design the ideal landscape in their minds using diagrams and a written description, with no limits imposed. Afterwards, the researcher was able to classify them into several preferred designs shown in the table with self explanation (Kongjian Yu, 1990) (table 1).

Table 1   The ideal landscape model of a dwelling from statistical psychology (Kongjian Yu, 1990).

The ideal landscape of a dwelling	feature description	preference rate (%)
A	"The house has a mountain at the back and water in the front, surrounded by trees." "The front has a view of lawn with lots of flowers and an expanse of water with ducks swimming in it. It is so refreshing." " A small path winds its way over the water and leads into the depth of the forest on the other side of the bank. You can swim in the water, rest on the lawn or have a walk in the forest."	72.4
B	"There is water between the house and the hills; the distant view is of a hill and forest and near the house, the reflection in the water can be appreciated. A small path goes over a bridge and leads its way into the forest."	10.3
C	"A small path winds its way through the forest and leads to a broad smooth expanse of water."	5.7
D	"I want my little house to have a hill at the back." "I would like a small forest in front of my house...with a small clear area in front for me to enjoy activities." "I prefer a winding path which climbs up the hill and leads to the outside world." "It would be ideal to have a clear stream running in front of the gate."	3.4
others		8.2

2.4 Feng-shui expresses the ideal pattern in the depths of Chinese hearts

The ideal landscape models discussed above were generated from various backgrounds but with some common structural features. If we consider the structure of "enclosure + entrance" as a gourd, then the Kunlun Mountain model is "a gourd on a high mountain," the Penglai model is "a floating gourd," Tao Yuanming's model is "a gourd with a stock," and the ideal livable model in landscape painting and statistical psychology is "a gourd in or at the foothill of mountains." The ideal Feng-shui model gathers together all the structural features of all the ideal models mentioned above (table 2) and makes up and strengthens a certain kind of structure by applying some meaningful symbols, such as a pavilion and pagoda, etc.

Except for the Feng-shui model, all the other ideal landscape models in table 2 are obviously beyond reality. No matter whether they have some kind of material and social utility or not, these ideal landscapes are all imaginative and unreachable, and they all seem to originate from the same pattern in the depths of Chinese hearts. Feng-shui theory indeed demonstrates this pattern and makes an effort to realize it in the real environment, hoping to achieve the most satisfaction in the pursuit of material utilitarian benefits in real society (such as the blessings of riches, long life, and many offsprings).

But the question is whether there exists any realistic relationship of structure and function between this ideal pattern (an ideal Feng-shui model) in the depths of Chinese hearts and the utilitarian purpose that Feng-shui theory aims to achieve in reality. Based on the philosophy of Qi, Feng-shui took living Qi as a kind of function current (Kongjian Yu, 1991), and set up the theory and technical system of investigating Qi by the landforms and judging the living Qi by the structure of the landscape. And obviously there is a lack of scientific proof and therefore a systematic misunderstanding (details later). It can't be taken seriously. Many modern scholars have tried to explain the Chinese people's dependence on the Feng-shui model with the relationship between a realistic ecological function of cultivation and the structure of Feng-shui. For

Table 2   Feng-shui expresses the ideal landscape pattern in the depth of Chinese hearts.

The ideal landscape model	main structural features	background
The Kunlun mountain model The Penglai model The Gourd space model	"A gourd in high mountains" (a steep rocky landform as a barrier +surrounding mountains as enclosure) "A floating gourd" (islands as a barrier + gourd mouth + gourd cavity) "A hanging gourd" (spatial separation + gourd mouth + gourd cavity)	a territory which can satisfy all physical and material desires (including gold, jade, beauty and the medicine of eternal life) but impossible to reach in reality.
Tao Yuanming's model The Mountain dwelling model	"A gourd with a stock" (corridor + entrance + basin enclosure) "A gourd in or near mountains" (forest enclosure and screening + steep rock or water surface as a barrier + windy corridor in the valley and entrance + the close to the edge feature of leaning on a mountain or water)	As the background of Utopian society, they are the dream dwelling places of the artists beyond the utilitarian and materialist interests of society
The ideal model of statistical psychology	"A gourd in or near mountains" (a forest enclosure and screening + a winding path corridor across the forest + the close to the edge feature of leaning on a mountain or water)	The dream of modern living landscape
The Feng-shui model	Includes all the ideal features mentioned above and makes up and strengthens some certain kind of structure by applying some artificial construction and meaningful symbols.	The dwelling of today and the future world which can bring the most social, material and utilitarian benefits

example, a house with hills behind it and water in front not only collects maximum sunlight, but also avoids suffering the cold north wind in winter, and enjoys the cool southern breeze in summer. In some areas, the explanations are acceptable. But the significance of the Feng-shui model can't be completely comprehended only through analyzing the relationship between a realistic ecological function of cultivation and the structure of Feng-shui. After all, the site ecology is not enough to explain the meaning of Feng-shui, there must be something else for the ideal Feng-shui of tomb siting.

(Except for the benefits in its own theory.)

No matter which angle you approach it from, a mountain basin with many layers of barriers and only a small entrance to connect it with the outside world does not really have advantages in cultivation ecology. The structure of an ideal Feng-shui model (the Chinese people's ideal landscape pattern) is like a code, and its deeper meaning cannot be gleaned from a superficial "literal meaning." So how can we know the hidden meaning of structures after all? In the following chapters, Yu will investigate the meaning beyond realistic utilitarian functions in the ideal Feng-shui model from the perspective of the bio-ecological adaptation in the process of human evolution, and from the relationship between the historical significance of ecological utilitarianism and the landscape structure.

3

From Marmot to Robinson Crusoe:

the instinct of choosing the right habitation

would like to start this chapter with Simonds's story "The Hunter and the Wise Man" (Simonds 1983, I).

One morning, a hunter and a young boy came into the middle of a grassland. They stared at a mound in front of them where they found some marmot holes (figure 55).

Figure 55   *A marmot and its habitation (picture taken by the author).*

"What a clever marmot," said the hunter. "They select their living places so carefully that whenever you see the marmot holes, you will always find a field of crops nearby so it makes it easy for them to look for food. And they are always close to streams or swamps for the convenience of water. They never settle their homes near willow trees or alder forests because some terrible natural enemies, such as owls and hawks, often make their habitation there. As well they do not build their homes in piles of rocks to avoid the hidden snakes, which are another kind of natural enemy to them. The marmots build their homes on the southeast slope of the mound where there is plenty of sunshine to keep their holes warm and comfortable. In winter, the soil on the northwest slope turns dry and hard due to the cold wind, while on the other side of the hill there is a thick layer of soft snow to cover the marmot homes. When they dig their holes, they first make a steep downward passage one to three feet deep. Then they take a U-turn to make a nest in the soil near the roots of the grass. Thus in winter they can avoid the cold wind and bask in the warm sunshine, and they do not have to go far for food and water while having each other's company. They do have a wonderful plan for their home."

"Is our town built on the southeast side of the hill?" the boy wondered.

"No." The hunter frowned and said, "Our town is on the northern slope of the hill and we suffer the cold wind in winter, and even in summer the cold breeze doesn't favor us. Our newly built linen factory, which is the only one within forty square miles, occupies the spot where the summer breeze comes into town, and black smoke from the factory is blown into the whole town and invades every open window."

"But at least our town is built on the riverbank so it's close to water!" the child argued.

"Yes," responded the hunter, "but that is the wrong way to be close to water—we are on the low point of the bank! Every summer, when the snow on the grassland melts, the water in the river rises and the basement of every house in town is soaked with floodwater."

"Marmots won't do that. They do a good job designing their home, and they seem to be even better at it than people."

"That's right," the hunter thought for a moment. "From what I know, most animals are like that. Sometimes I feel it's strange and wonder why."

Simonds's story is a bit sad, and also ironic, given that people, with their modern civilization, consider themselves to be the top species among all the creatures.

3.1 The revelation of animal choices for habitation

What kind of a place should be chosen for habitation? How to get food? How to avoid encountering natural enemies, and what strategy to adopt for multiplying? Most animals must solve these problems. Whether it finds a successful habitat will decide to a great extent the results of these three actions, and may finally lead the species to prosper or die out. A certain kind of habitat means a certain kind of environmental condition, which forces the animal to be under the pressure of natural selection. Therefore, different choices of habitation among the same species can cause regional differences. And the different choices and adaptation of habitations among different species will strengthen genetic diversity (Partridge, 1978). When it chooses a habitation, the animal also has a chance to remold itself. Inherited instincts cause the animal to have a special preference for a certain kind of habitat. In other words, through genes, ancestors have already set an ideal habitat model for their descendants. At the same time, when faced with real conditions, the animal can adapt to a new environment to a certain extent through its learning experiences, as well as constructing the ideal model that is set in its genes. Much outdoor observation and work in laboratories has proved that, based on inherited instincts, animals can make an effort to choose their own kind of ideal or nearly ideal habitation.

The determining conditions for an animal's ideal habitat are an abundant supply of food, the safety of avoiding natural enemies, and the ability to multiply and raise their young efficiently. But in many situations, these final determining factors are very hard to assess during the process of choosing the right place to live. And this requires the animal to choose a place to live from a long-term view by environmental signs that can be perceived in the situation. Some of these environmental factors, which are considered the basis for habitation selection, are often quite different from the ideal goal, and sometimes the animal has to sacrifice temporary gain in order to meet long-term needs. This often happens especially to seasonal animals. Natural selection has endowed animals with this ability. Animals like the marmots mentioned above usually take food and water resources as direct guidance in achieving the final goal of habitat selection. But for some individuals who don't have experience choosing a safe living environment for winter, the instinctive reaction to indirect landscape features will work for them (figure 56)— the northwest slope = cold winter; piles of rock = ferocious snakes; willow or alder forest = predatory owls and hawks.

When selecting habitat, animals are not only very discerning, but also sometimes have to spend a great deal of time and energy in changing the environment to make their living place more like the ideal model. Beavers' dam-building behavior is well known to us. They even to some degree change the structure of the river system (Marsh, 1965; Cronon, 1984). In a situation where resources are limited and regionally restricted, an animal's territory-protecting behavior will manifest itself, and its habitat will become a territory in which others are completely excluded. They claim and protect their territories using all sorts of signs (visual, olfactory, or audio), and are ready to attack invaders at any time. As both human beings and animals, how do we choose, remake, and protect our living places?

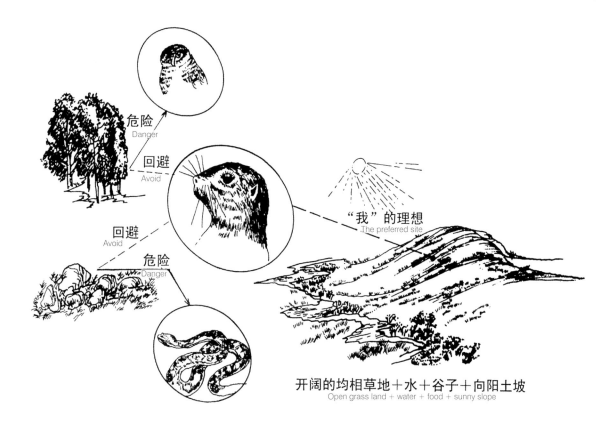

危险
Danger

回避
Avoid

回避
Avoid

危险
Danger

"我" 的理想
The preferred site

开阔的均相草地＋水＋谷子＋向阳土坡
Open grass land + water + food + sunny slope

Figure 56   A marmot's reaction to the landscape features in its environment (illustrated by the author).

3.2 Seeing the human gift for habitation selection through Robinson Crusoe's choice of dwellings

As human beings, when compared with animals in the selection and design of habitation, we don't have to be like the mocked "civilized people" in Simonds's story, who were incapable and passive. On the contrary, if we compare only our ability to select, and not that of reforming or creating, human beings are wiser, more critical, and have more taboos.

In modern civilization, all animal nature in human actions is covered with a thick layer of culture dust, making it difficult for people to figure out whether we are a kind creature with a special nature or a machine under the control of culture. But when humans are cast into nature, all of their biological particularities are fully demonstrated. Most people don't get a chance to experience this directly in their lives, so Daniel Defoe, the British novelist, used Robinson Crusoe to make a somewhat realistic portrayal and expose the secrets of human nature. Crusoe, a businessman of a civilized age, struggled to live for twenty-eight years after he survived a shipwreck and landed on an isolated island where no other human was to be found. The first thing he did after he crawled ashore was to look for a place to live. Let us have a look at how human nature manifested itself (from *Robinson Crusoe*):

After he pulled himself together, Crusoe began to look around to see what kind of place he was in and what was the next thing to be done. Soon he realized he was in a wild place where he could find nothing to eat or drink to comfort himself. The shade of night started to creep in. When he thought that soon he might become some wild beast's prey, his heart sank. "All the remedy that offered to my thoughts, at that time, was, to get up into a thick bushy tree, like a fir, but thorny— which grew near me, and where I resolved to sit all night—and consider the next day (chapter 3).

Soon thereafter, the most important thing for him to do was to look for a place to stay.

My thoughts were now wholly employed about securing myself against either savages, if any should appear, or wild beasts, if any were in the island … I consulted several things in my situation, which I found would be proper for me: first, health and fresh water … secondly, shelter from the heat of the sun; thirdly, security from ravenous creatures, whether man or beast; fourthly, a view to the sea, that if God sent any ship in sight, I might not lose any advantage for my deliverance, for which I was not willing to banish all my expectation yet.

In search of a place proper for this, I found a little plain on the side of a rising hill, whose front towards this little plain was steep as a house side, so that nothing could come down upon me from the top. On the side of this rock there was a hollow place, worn a little way in like the entrance or door of a cave, but there was not really any cave, or way into the rock, at all. On the flat of the green, just before this hollow place, I resolved to pitch my tent. This plain was not above a hundred yards broad, and about twice as long, and lay like a green before my door; and, at the end of it, descended irregularly every way down into the low grounds by the seaside. It was on the north-north-west side of the hill, so that it was sheltered from the heat every day (chapter 5) (figure 57).

After he decided on the foundation of the living place, Crusoe set up a double-layered fence that was a semicircle ten yards in diameter, with the shallow cave at its center. The fence and cliff together formed an entirely sealed habitat that had no entrance except for a wooden ladder that allowed him to go in and out. Upon later exploration of the island, he found another habitat in the forest with more readily available food, but further from the shore. He built his "country villa" there. Crusoe's actions in habitation selection reveal certain kinds of psychological characteristics in human beings. This is why *Robinson Crusoe* strikes a dramatic resonance in people; his desires and behavior were just like everyone else's, that is, a feature of human biological makeup.

Figure 57   A diagram of Crusoe's satisfactory habitation (illustrated according to Robinson Crusoe).

The satisfactory model of primitive Chinese habitations

4.1 From forest to forest grasslands— the developing process of sensing good and bad environments

We can see from chapter 3 that, as human beings, we are very concerned with details when we choose an ideal living place, and our ability to cognize landscape is no lower than that of other animals. Based on the principles of evolution and natural selection, this indicates that we humans once experienced rigorous trials and strict natural selection.

About 1.5 million years ago, the effect of glaciers caused the earth to gradually turn cold and dry. The original closed Miocene forest landscape, with relatively even landscapes in many parts of the old continents (mainly Asia, Africa, and Europe), changed into open forest with various kinds of grassland landscape. As an inferior specimen among the forest apes, our primitive human ancestors had to leave the dense forests, giving up their homes in trees in the tropical jungles of Africa and settling on the ground. And there the doleful history of human evolution and development commenced. Some evidence shows that, about three to four million years ago, during a period lasting more than ten million years, the distribution of our primitive human ancestors was mainly limited to the savanna landscape in Africa (tropical grasslands with scattered trees).

Figure 58   Maasai Mara National Reserve, Kenya, the kind of landscape that Homo sapiens is believed to get evolved, where challenges and opportunities coexist for Homo sapiens both as hunter and be hunted, and according to Appleton's theory (1975), the landscape is perceived as prospect or refuge (photo by the author).

Figure 59   A single tree on the open grassland has meaning of life and death to the Homo Sapiens who plays both as hunter and/or pray (Maasai Mara National Reserve, Kenya, Photo by the author).

Compared with life in the trees in hot, damp forests, early Homo sapiens faced much greater challenges in the savanna landscape. In fact, both dangers and opportunities co-existed at the same time. On the one hand, there were abundant resources for hunting on the grasslands where herbivores were plentiful. Perennial plants and small animals that lived on the sides of rivers could be collected for food. On the other hand, life down on the ground meant that our early ancestors had to live on the same activity level as ferocious animals like lions and hyaenidae, which lived in the grasslands. Homo sapiens now became the prey of other creatures. Life was different from their ancestors when they lived in trees high above other animal hunters and could jump from one tree to another, enjoying the richness of fruit and tender leaves as their food. In the hot, damp jungle, there was usually a lack of spatial structure in the landscape. Thick branches and leaves made it possible for creatures that lived in trees to have all their activities occur in hidden places. Even when they were actually very close to each other, they were not noticeable. Therefore, it was inefficient to sense the landscape visually, and they developed the ability to read the landscape and recognize each other mainly through listening and smelling. Hiding and reducing the sound of their activities became the direction of evolution for most jungle animals. But in the grasslands, with only scattered trees, there were diverse spatial settings in a landscape, and hidden dangers everywhere in the tall grass, bushes, in the water, and behind rocks. Our human ancestors could see prey and other hunters in the distance on the horizon, but at the same time they themselves were easily exposed to the prey and other hunters. Our ancestors needed to be able to make quick, precise judgments regarding an object that suddenly appeared in their sight, in order to react by fight or flight. This led to the development of human visual acuity. If we compare humans with the species of the primates who were never able to walk out of the forest, we will see that the experience of the savanna landscape, which lasted some ten million years and took up most of human evolutionary history, played an incredible role in the evolution and formation of our physical and psychological structure.

If we only consider physical condition, humankind is indeed an inferior species. We are slower runners than hoofed animals; we can't beat carnivorous animals in a fight; we aren't as fast at tree climbing as other kinds of primates; if we fall into water, we aren't good swimmers; and we don't have a thick layer of fur and fat to protect us from cold, like some other kinds of animals. But it is also because of these physical disadvantages that human beings were forced to develop and survive through choosing special habitations and by making the best use of the natural landscape. Our living places and environmental conditions had to effectively meet the needs listed below.

4.1.1 Shelter

After our human ancestors came down to live on the ground, they had to be able to use some structures in the landscape to escape predators. Fossil evidence shows that the Homo sapiens who lived on the African grasslands survived their natural enemies mainly by climbing up trees and rocks (see Geist, 1978). In the long period of time after our early ancestors gave up living in trees, they still wandered along the edges of forests and kept a certain distance from forests and cliffs in order to climb up trees or rocks before the wild beasts of the grasslands got too close. Under the pressure of cruel natural selection, being close to the edge was obviously a valuable form of adaptation. In the vast, empty grasslands where the forest margin or rocky cliffs were at a distance, even if one or two lonely trees or some steep rocks could provide security and something to depend on in the process of exploiting the grassland, they might become the central point of our ancestors' activity area. It was the climbing ability inherited from the experience of living in trees that enabled our ancestors to form a spatial separation and make good use of trees and steep rocks in order to avoid attack from carnivores with little climbing ability. Remember, the first night after Crusoe survived the storm and came ashore he slept in a tree.

Homo sapiens had to spend long, cold nights in total darkness where they couldn't see the approaching ferocious animals (this is the very reason why human beings fear darkness). It wasn't enough to temporarily avoid being chased by other hunters just by climbing up trees and rocks.

They needed to have a relatively safe and stable place to live as their primary habitation. Caves and platforms on rock cliffs were usually the best choices for building a closed barrier to keep some carnivores and human adversaries from gaining access. To fierce animals and competitors, an unsure shelter was a potentially dangerous place. With an extremely limited ability to use tools, being close to a landscape that provided separation, such as a river or a cliff, was very advantageous to our ancestors in building highly efficient shelters. Crusoe's behavior in selecting a living place was a vivid demonstration of this.

4.1.2 Hunting

We have reason to believe that our human ancestors who lived on the grasslands adopted many kinds of hunting methods. From basic Opportunistic hunting in the beginning, to the planned hunting that later developed into cooperative hunting, ambush hunting, etc. (Geist, 1978)—no matter the method, they were all carried out by taking advantage of the natural landscape to some degree. Opportunistic hunting mainly consisted of visiting the places where prey was captured, or animal habitats, such as a cave. This required that primitive people be able to gauge the whole situation and judge whether the prey was available by reading all sorts of signs in the landscape. Planned hunting entailed approaching prey quietly and killing it suddenly before it noticed any danger. Humans' thick, soft soles are probably an adaptation from this kind of hunting behavior (Geist, 1978). Obviously, some landscape features between the hunter and the prey (such as huge rocks or bushes) providing a hiding place but not preventing approaching the prey, were able to greatly improve the efficiency of planned hunting. In cooperative hunting, our human ancestors learned to use natural traps such as cliffs and swamps. They purposely chased some herbivorous animals, sometimes even huge animals like mammoths, off a cliff or into a swamp. Archaeologists have found that Neanderthals who lived between 400,000 and 40,000 years were experts at hunting this way. They usually set up their habitations near cliffs or other natural barriers (Clork 1970, 142). Ambush hunting took even more advantage of the landscape structure. Hunters hid in places where they knew they would encounter migrating animals, or near resources such as water, waiting for an opportune moment to attack. In this kind of hunting, an entrance (mouth of a barrier) and a corridor were the most effective landscape structures, and this obviously has guided humankind to have a special preference for this kind of structure (Kongjian Yu, 1990).

4.1.3 Environmental discrimination and exploration

Primitive people, as both hunter and hunted, not only had to decide whether things that appeared in the landscape were good or bad, but also had to make the right judgment as to the environment itself. In the cruel hunting age, to lose your way was tantamount to walking into death. But the human ability for environmental discrimination pales in comparison with that of other animals, such as hunting dogs, messenger pigeons, or migrating birds that cross continents and oceans and come back to the very same spot the next year. In this area, humankind's ability cannot even be compared with rats, and this meant that people had to be more discriminating in their choice of landscape. Therefore, those environmental cognition features, such as the holistic spatial patterns and measurements of the landscape, and features that are helpful for positioning and orientation, undoubtedly became the conditions for choosing habitations and activity spaces.

In their long experience of living in forests and grasslands, primitive people never stopped exploring new landscapes and new habitations. It was this human drive to explore and exploit that enabled us to conquer every corner of the earth, and even outer space. A habitat with no potential for exploration and development will lead a whole group of individuals to death when there is a crisis of dry out of resources and the group expands beyond the carrying capacity of the habitat. Thus, a landscape structure that signifies the potential for spatial and future development will become one of the necessary conditions for humankind's habitation selection.

4.1.4 Guarding territory

The long process of Homo sapiens' evolution covered the period of the extensive spread of grasslands, the ice climate when herbivorous animals multiplied greatly, the regression of the grasslands, desert invasion of forests, and the ice age when resources were extremely reduced. During the latter period, hunting resources became scarce and were mainly scattered along the banks of rivers and swamps and in some valley basins. This caused dramatic competition among Homo sapiens, leading to the emergence of a kind of territory that completely excluded other groups of Homo sapiens. Due to this, humankind's territory-protecting behavior started to develop. The limitations, uneven distribution, and the possibility of keeping natural resources were the basic conditions for territory-guarding behavior to develop. The territory occupier had to sacrifice part of his energy to patrol, mark, and protect his territory, in order to keep the rights to the resource. But if the distribution of resources in the habitation was scattered, it would cause the spatial measurements of the habitation to be too big, or make it difficult to mark and patrol the territory. When the protecting structure was weak, the occupiers had to spend too much energy guarding the territory and the loss would be greater than the gain. That was why primitive people favored a landscape with a concentrated distribution of resources that was easier to guard.

To summarize, after the ancestors of humankind came down from the trees and moved into a variety of landscapes in forests and grasslands, they had to face cruel natural selection, and thus a series of adaptive actions evolved. In addition, the mental abilities of landscape cognition and judging developed. This enabled humankind to take advantage of some of the structures of natural landscapes to overcome their physical and physiological disadvantages, so that they could effectively take refuge, hunt for food, discriminate between environments, explore and exploit new areas, and guard their habitations in order to keep the resources to themselves. And landscape structures that helped humankind achieve the actions mentioned above became the ideal habitation features that people depended on to survive and develop, as well as being what they preferred and pursued (figures 60, 61, 62 and 63). On this basis, let's take a look at primitive Chinese people's ideal model of habitation and its structural features.

Figure 61 A landscape which is lacking a discriminating structure causes peoples' spatial movement to lose direction (photo taken by the author).

Figure 60 Children's like for climbing trees originated from the adaptation to hunting and seeking shelter (photo taken by the author).

Figure 62 People's taste in territory structure originated from the adaptation to territory guarding (photo taken by the author).

Figure 63 The attraction to watch and peep originated from the adaptation to environmental discrimination and exploration (photo taken by the author).

4.2 The ideal habitat model of primitive Chinese people—the original form of ideal Feng-shui

After surviving a more than ten-million-year period of natural selection in tropical grasslands with scattered trees (forest grasslands) in Africa, in the early part of the Pleistocene (about three million years ago), our human ancestors appeared on the Eurasian continent with the physical and mental particularity of standing upright. The Homo erectus that appeared on Chinese soil found themselves in a complicated landscape from the very beginning. From the discovered habitation remains of primitive people in China, we can see that most of them, from Homo erectus to the late stage of Homo sapiens, were mainly scattered in three natural geographical areas—the eastern monsoon climate zone, the northwestern arid zone, and the transitional zone on the edge of the Tsinghai-Tibet alpine climate area (*History of Chinese Civilization*).

In these transition zones, mountains wound up and down and rivers crossed through them. Many different kinds of landscape provided varied choices for habitation to primitive Chinese people. Through the comparison and analysis of some typical long-term habitations of the primitive Chinese (table 3), we come across some "satisfactory habitations," referring to those better ones among the available choices for habitation at that time which were closest to the ideal model. Therefore, from these typically satisfactory habitations, we can see the ideal habitation model in primitive people's heart. And at the same time we can discern the ideal model that was handed down by ancestors to their descendants, even to modern people, because of primitive people's adaptation to the satisfactory yet not ideal habitation.

It is not difficult to see that there are obvious similar structural features among primitive Chinese people's satisfactory habitation, the ideal Feng-shui model, and the ideal landscape model of Chinese people expressed by the ideal Feng-shui model. Based on the discussion in the last paragraph of primitive people's activities seeking

Table 3　The typical structure of Chinese primitive people's satisfying habitations

the primitive people	the entire landscape structure of the habitation
Yuanmou man (early stage of homo erectus, about 1.7 million years ago)	The habitation is located in Yuanmou basin. It covers 30 kilometres from the north to the south and is 7 kilometres in width. The fossils were discovered in a small hill at the foot of Dongshan Mountain in the basin, which is 4 metres above the basin and covers only 320 square metres. The area near the hill is on higher ground with the relative height of about 150m. The entire topography is slanting from the east to the southwest and northwest directions. Bang River is on the southwest of the basin and flows into Longchuan River before it joins Jinsha River.
Lantian Man (early stage of homo erectus, about 1 million years ago)	The habitation is located in the valley of Ba River in the southeast corner of Guanzhong basin. The high Qinling mountains are to the southeast and abrupt loess plateaus are situated on both north and south sides. The fossils were discovered right next to a belt-like hillock at the northern foot of the Qinling mountains. The front edge of the hillock faces Ba River and is about 100 metres higher than the riverbed. Ba River flows out from the southeast of the Qinling mountains into the plain on the rift valley of Wei River (figure 64).
Peking Man (homo erectus stage, about 200-700 thousand years ago)	The habitation is in the Zhoukoudian area located in the northwest corner of the great Huabei plain. It leans on a range of high mountains to the northwest with rolling hills to the northeast. To the south and southeast the great Huabei plain slants slowly to the south.There is a relatively independent hill in front of Dragonbone Mountain on the northwest foot of the high mountains. Dragonbone cave on the mountain, was the direct living environment of Peking man. Nearby, Ba'er River overlooks a corner of the great plain which has a relative height of about 70 metres. Ba'er River flows through Liuli River and Yongding River before it joins the corridor of Sanggan River (figure 65).
The Maba people (early homo sapiens, about100 thousand years ago)	The habitation is located in the basin of lime stone mountains in Maba, Guangdong. Lion Mountain, where the cave was found, is an isolated peak of limestone 60-70 metres in height. It is surrounded by lower hills. Maba River winds its way in the basin and later joins Beijiang River. The cave overlooks the basin and the surrounding swamps (figures 66 and 67).
The Small Nanhai Culture (about 13-25 thousand years ago)	Culture site is 25 kilometres to the west of Anyang city and is located in the transition area between Taihang Mountain range on the west side and Huabei plain on the east side. The primitive people's cave is in a basin, which covers 3 square kilometers and connects with the great Huabei plain by the Wanquan River. The basin is located in the middle of the north mountains, facing east and overlooking smaller valley basins (figures 68 and 69).
The upper Cave Man (late homo sapiens, about 10 thousand years ago)	Similar to the landscape of the habitation of Peking Man.

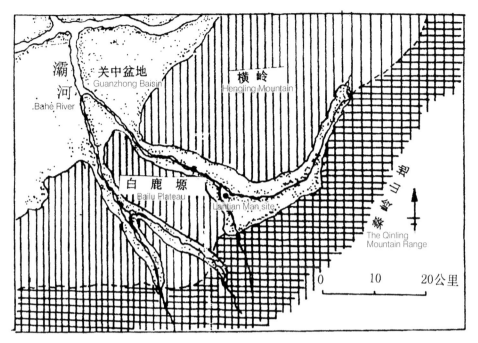

Figure 64   The entire landscape structure of Lantian Man's habitation (Kongjian Yu, 1990).

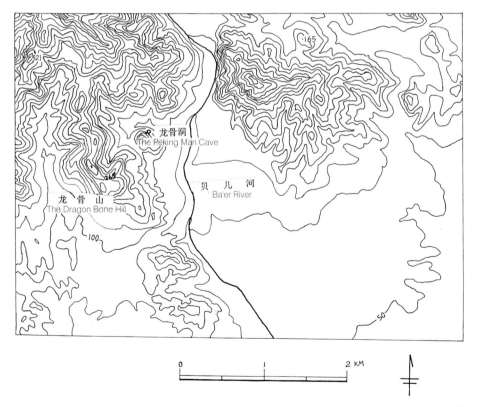

Figure 65   The entire landscape structure of Peking Man's habitation (Kongjian Yu, 1990).

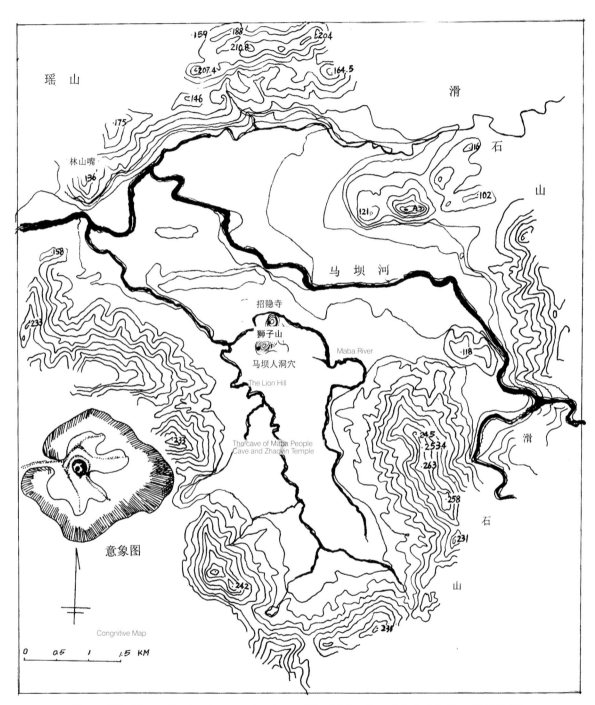

瑶 山

滑 石 山

马 坝 河

招隐寺
狮子山
马坝人洞穴

Maba River

The Lion Hill

The cave of Maba People
Cave and Zhaoyin Temple

滑 石 山

意象图

Congnitive Map

0   0.5   1   1.5 KM

Figure 66   The entire landscape structure of the Maba People's habitation (1:50,000 to the real topography).

Figure 67   The landscape of the Maba People's habitation (photo taken by the author).

Figure 68   The landscape of the site of the Small Nanhai Culture (photo taken by the author).

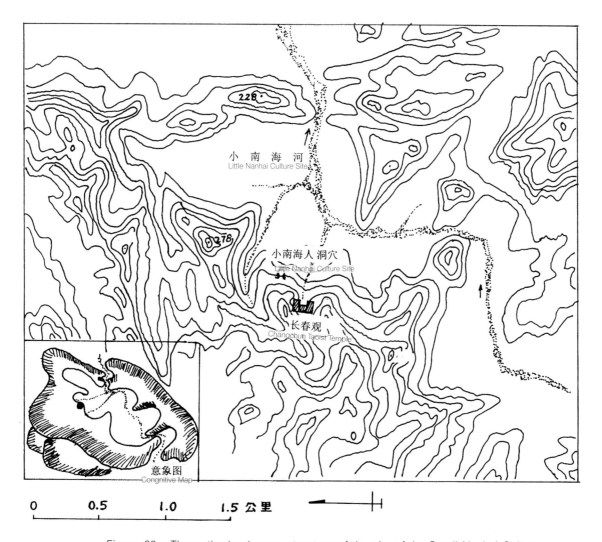

Figure 69   The entire landscape structure of the site of the Small Nanhai Culture (according to the survey of the site, 1:50,000 to the real topography).

shelter, hunting, discriminating between environments, and exploring and guarding territory, we are going to analyze the main ecological functions of the landscape structure of the satisfactory habitations mentioned above.

4.2.1 The effects of enclosures and measurements

The typical satisfactory habitations in table 3 were all located in a hilly basin, a river valley, or the corner of a plain, and they all feature some kind of enclosure. Their spatial measurements are within a certain range and visually form a landscape unit with a strong unified sense that was the usual area for hunting and gathering food. This entire space, with a relatively even landscape in controlable sizes held a series of ecological meanings and effects for primitive people.

First, some research shows that the best number for a cooperative group among individuals is 5 + 2, which is called the magic number. A primitive people's hunting group was most commonly five people (Geist, 1978). Usually a group of primitive people who lived together comprised ten to twelve adults, and, counting children, numbered about twenty to twenty-five people. Obviously it was not an easy thing for a group of about five people to hunt, stay safe, or guard territory in a vast grassland. For hunting, they had to prevent the prey from escaping from any corner, and for staying safe they had to watch in all directions for sudden attack. So if they had an environment where a cliff could be used as a screen to form a fence or something that came close to being a fence, these activities could be more easily carried out.

Second, from the very beginning, people were not capable of walking long distances. Taking the living site or the cave as the center, their usual activities were all within a ten-kilometer range. Anything further than this, and the energy spent walking might exceed the energy gained in the hunt, which would make the hunting uneconomic. No matter what the area, climate, or resources were like, measuring a hunting range in this way, resources can only carry a load of about twenty-five people (Jiyi Pan, 1988). Therefore, a closed environment of this size is compatible with a primitive people's ideal group size, resource requirements, their ability to guard territory, and their ability to move. The effects of measurement have long-lasting meaning.

Third, as stated above, people's environmental discrimination ability was very limited. Therefore, a closed area with a clear boundary and measurement limit could keep their hunting activity within a space where boundaries were clear and familiar, and the ecological relationship was relatively well known. The up-and-down outline of mountains at the boundary and the features of landscape became references for hunters to position themselves. If they walked out of these references, they might get lost and become a meal for some carnivore.

Fourth, an already occupied enclosure could cause problems for invaders who might not only be attacked at any time but could also find themselves trapped and unable to escape. Therefore, the same enclosure space could offer totally different landscape senses to the owner and to a new invader.

Fifth, a basin or river valley enclosure usually had a good micro climate that contributed to the abundance and regeneration of resources.

4.2.2 The edge effects

Each typical habitation mentioned above had the attribute of "being close to the edge," because they were all located in the edge areas of their own ecological system, such as the interlocking areas of hills, plains, basins, and river valleys. And caves, the direct living environment of primitive people, also had the advantage of being situated along the edges of mountains. This caused a series of effects of "being close to the edge":

First, the clear transitional features of temperature, dampness, and the type of soil on edge zones caused the emergence of many varieties of transitional vegetation and thus became gathering areas for various herbivorous animals. This provided abundant resources for primitive people's hunting and food collection.

Second, the edge zones in these geographical landscapes were often necessary paths for migrating animals, such as herbivorous animals that migrated between mountains and plains. Some migration happened due to the animals' need for a variety of ecological systems. The edge zones provided great places and opportunities for hunting.

Third, edge zones provided the convenience of "prospect—refuge" which was crucial to primitive people in a drastically competitive environment (Appleton, 1975). On one hand, people had to watch everything all the time to notice anything happening, including the movements of enemies and the tracking of prey. On the other hand, due to the limitations of human visual range, people had to make sure that they were safe from behind and were able to attack or escape accordingly. A habitation at foothill, leaning on a high mountain overlooking a plain, which "could see others but could not be seen," was the ideal position for both guarding and attacking.

Fourth, landscape heterogeneity caused by edge zones of various landscapes were of significant value in environmental discrimination.

4.2.3 The effects of separation

In addition to a landscape isolated from an entire view formed by a closed structure leaning on a mountain and facing water, the direct living environment of primitive Chinese people, that is, the cave and its surroundings, was very important. A cave had to be absolutely secure. Therefore, the direct living environment was neither on a tall mountain, nor on a broad empty plain, but on a relatively independent hill or an isolated peak near a tall mountain, where both the height and area were limited. The features of this kind of landscape had the following effects:

First, within the restricted range of this area, any potential danger could be eliminated.

Second, although the direct living environment was in a much lower position than the closed topography structure on the edge of the habitation, it was the vantage point in the area of habitation and overlooked the landscape with the strategic advantage of attacking from a high position.

Third, the relatively independent landscape unit (just like a tree or a rock standing by itself), which contrasted with the entire matrix landscape in size and shape, became the main environmental markers. And they were also important anchor points in primitive people's environmental cognition pattern.

4.2.4 The effects of entrances and corridors

Satisfactory enclosures weren't completely closed, and they were all connected with the outside world by entrances that usually formed corridors along rivers and mountain valleys. This kind of landscape structure had some of the following effects:

First, entrances and corridors were the communication channels for materials, energy, and information with the outside world, and also the necessary paths for the spatial movements of the species. Due to having the highest density of resources and the richest kinds of species, entrances and corridors were the best places for gathering and especially for hunting. In the dry seasons, an entrance (water mouth) and a corridor might become the only place for water, animals, and tender plants. A corridor, which was made by animals treading through the grass and bushes, also suggested water resources and prey.

Second, they played a key role in guarding territory, and had the strategic advantage of "guarding the gate with one man." In this regard, a corridor strengthened the defensive advantage of an entrance, putting intruders at a strategic disadvantage for a longer time and in a bigger area. Once the intruders broke through the entrance and the corridor, it would be difficult to guard the territory. Therefore, in some sense, gaining or losing control of the entrance and corridor decided the fate of the habitation.

Third, the occupiers of an entrance could not be seen when spying on others. They could maintain the secrecy of their habitation or refuge and at the same time watch for movements outside and prepare to attack or defend. In this sense, the entrance structure of a habitation was just like the peephole in the door of a modern urban apartment.

Fourth, an entrance and a corridor were passages for primitive tribes to explore and exploit new space. When the population expanded and resources dried up, a tribe could extend through the entrance or along the corridor to new habitations in order to ensure its continued development. For example, Peking Man abandoned their habitations in the

Dragonbone Mountain area many times, and it is very likely that they followed the Yongding River, and the valley corridor of Sanggan River into the valley basins in Hebei and Shanxi Provinces (Lanpo Jia, Weiwen Huang, 1984).

Fifth, a corridor and an entrance were not just a passage and an exit. They were also the basic structures for spatial discrimination, and could keep primitive people from getting lost while hunting or migrating. They connected the past, present, and future, and were the key crunodes and lines in a spatial cognition pattern.

In short, while allowing the territory owner freedom of movement and exploration in the environment, entrances and corridors maintained all the effects of a closed structure, and acted as highly concentrated gathering places for materials, energy, and bio-diversity. They also played a key role in environmental discrimination and territory guarding.

We can see that satisfactory habitations of primitive Chinese people had many kinds of ecological effects, and that their landscape structures offered them a strategic advantage in territory guarding, taking refuge, hunting, environmental discrimination, exploration, and exploitation of new spaces. Whether a habitation with ecological effects could be found successfully was a kind of selective pressure on the evolution and development of humankind. Natural selection and experience inheritance kept primitive people's ability for habitation selection eternally set in their biological genes. After the Chinese nation entered its cultivation period, mental capacity that had evolved and developed during the times of hunting and gathering had already lost its original ecological utility in many cases. But it was unconsciously manifested in people's cognitive processes regarding landscape, and was demonstrated in the attraction of good or bad fortune to the characteristics of landscape structure. We can't use realistic, utilitarian, logical relationships to explain attracting good or bad fortune to a landscape that was subconsciously controlled. Thus it is still a mystery. And it is this attraction of good or bad fortune that formed the very deep, basic structure of Chinese people's sense of good or bad landscape (the sense of Feng-shui).

If we compare the satisfactory habitations of the primitive Chinese with the ideal Feng-shui model and other ideal landscape models, we find the phenomenon that they all have the same structure. In fact, on the isolated peak of Lion Rock Hill, a former Maba people habitation, there was a "Zhaoyin" temple hidden in a cave where the sixth patriarch of Zen retreated to meditate before he went to Caoxi in south China to build his temple (figure 67). The site of Changchun Temple (construction began in the Tang Dynasty), where the Xiaoanhai Culture originated, was also located on a primitive people's habitation (figure 70). This was not a coincidence. The inheritance of experience had already firmly built an ideal model of habitation in the biological genes of the Chinese people.

Based on the discussion above, in the ideal Feng-shui model, the deep meaning in the features of the entire landscape structure, such as enclosure and screening, being close to the edge, leaning on water or a mountain, separation and being at a placenta-kind of location, and entrances and corridors, are clear. These gave the Chinese primitive

Figure 70   The site of Zhaoyin Temple was located on the Maba people habitation (photo taken by the author).

people's actions of taking refuge, hunting, environmental discrimination and exploration, and territory guarding obvious strategic advantages. On this basis, we will not find it difficult to understand the deep meanings of some small objects and symbols in the Feng-shui model.

4.3 Small Feng-shui objects

Compared with the features of an entire landscape structure, small objects and symbols were usually given more mysterious symbolic meanings. It would be helpful for us to further understand the deep meaning of the Feng-shui model if we study these small objects and symbols from the viewpoint of evolutionary history, which originated from primitive people's ecological experience and the mechanism of inducing good or bad landscapes.

4.3.1 Pavilions and pagodas

Feng-shui pavilions and pagodas are everywhere in ancient Chinese lands and they have numerous superficial meanings in Feng-shui culture. They are used either for block off fierce, evil spirits, or for reviving the community intellectually, gathering Qi to fill a gap or inspire lives. Similar to what is written in the Inscription of the Pavilion and Pagoda of the Divine Spring in Huilai, Guangdong: "People believe it is a splendid land. Most of the mountains here are high and lush in vegetation and undoubtedly they are designed and made by Heaven and Earth. If there was any defect, it has been repaired by man's work, which has added a unique character to it. The land contains the magnificent Qi of the universe and gathers wind and rain, thus naturally people are in unity with heaven … After the foundation of the pavilion was established, [people] stood on it and looked around. They found it isolated with no supporting company and moreover the sea was rolling and the mountain where the town lay was not high enough. Furthermore, the topography was too plain and the Qi was not completely strong. Therefore, a pagoda was built to its left, which could calm the sea nearby and promote the strength of the mountain in the distance and form a natural harmony with the pagodas in the county, as if they are greeting each other." Another example is Wenchang

Pagoda in Jingde, Anhui Province. The overall terrain of Huilai County (prefecture) was like "five tortoises coming out of their caves." If a tortoise walked away, it would have taken away the Qi of wealth and political success. In the prefecture, there were often fire disasters, and people believed Zhi Mountain in the southwest of the county was to blame for this, due to its flamelike shape. Therefore, a pagoda was built to "calm the tortoises" and "press down the fires" (Zhewen Luo, 1985). In fact, all these various meanings of Feng-shui culture were only the explanations people gave to symbols, such as pavilions and pagodas. But the virtuous meanings could only be found in the landscape experience of primitive people's habitations.

First, the meanings given by Feng-shui reflect the dependence and preference human genes have for environmental markers. A relatively even landscape that lacked natural markers meant there was a danger of getting lost. In this sense, a Feng-shui pagoda was no different from a tree standing alone on grassland, the abrupt apex of a mountain, or a huge rock that contrasts with the landscape. These were all crunodes in the patterns of environmental cognition.

Second, the Feng-shui pagoda laid claim to a territory and the materialized action of guarding it. In a sense, it played a similar role to the dung and piles of dry twigs that a lion uses to demarcate its territory on African grasslands, or the claw marks of a Bengali tiger on trees in an Indian jungle. These signify security for the owners of the territories and warnings and fear for intruders.

Third, a pagoda is the materialized action of watching and protecting. Whether a pagoda's watching function (including adversaries and landscape) is realized or not, its virtual meaning still shows people's preference for watching and spying. A pagoda, which normally appears at a village entrance, hilltop, or the entrance of strong fortresses (water mouth), is the materialized action of environmental spying without sacrificing the safety of the shelter (figure 72). In this sense, its function was the same as sentry posts located at the periphery of the living places of primitive tribes.

Fourth, a Feng-shui pagoda had the function of perfecting according to Gestalt psychology. Hunting experiences molded a complete, ideal habitation model in human genes. But in a real natural landscape, this model couldn't always be completely realized. Therefore, a Feng-shui pagoda could be used to mend the defect in a natural structure and mentally construct a complete ideal habitation.

Figure 71   The outlet water mouth enforced with pavilions and entrance gate (Linshan Village, Huizhou, Anhui Province, Photo by the author).

Figure 72   One of the deep meanings of pagodas: a materialized action of prying. Guoqing temple is hidden behind the pagoda (photo taken by the author).

4.3.2 Gate, memorial archway, and reflecting wall

Feng-shui theory pays special attention to these kinds of structures and treats them as keys for leading the living Qi and shunning and evicting evil spirits. Gates and bridges basically share the same meaning. They can be used for spatial enclosure and separation while still maintaining the convenience of people's movement in the environment. Some village gates, bridges, and memorial archways are the material representations of territory declaration and guarding (figures 73 and 74). A screen wall plays the same role as the front hill of a building location in Feng-shui structure in keeping the habitation or the direct living environment in a mysterious state that gives warning and fear to any intruders, be they humans or animals, who dare not hastily enter a shelter they are unsure of.

Figure 73   The village gate: A materialized action of territory declaration and guarding (Yunduan village on Qiqiao Mountain) (photo taken by the author).

4.3.3 Feng-shui trees and Feng-shui forests

In the vast countryside of southeast China, it is rare to find a village without a Feng-shui tree and a Feng-shui forest, and usually the age of the tree is the same as the village. Even in extreme poverty or in dire need of wood for fire, not one leaf of the tree can be picked (figures 76 and 77). The superficial meaning of Feng-shui is for gathering Qi and hiding breath, while the practical meaning in ecology is to retain water and soil and to prevent wind and sun damage. But the deeper significance is the tree's role as a spatial screen and as an environmental marker in the cognition map of the local people. At the same time, a Feng-shui tree and a Feng-shui forest also exist as potential shelters, and this function obviously surpasses their practical ecological utility. Furthermore, they are the outcome of Chinese cultural and ecological prudent behavior, and the relic of an ecological adaptation mechanism in Chinese basin culture (Yu, 1991, 1992).

Figure 74   The memorial archway: A materialized action of territory declaration and guarding (Wannan, photo taken by the author).

Figure 75   Feng-shui forest in front of a village acts like a screen break to visually protecting the occupants (Xunjiansi, WuyanCountry•Jiangxi Province).

Figure 76   A Feng-shui forest (photo taken by the author).

Figure 77   A Feng-shui tree and its guarding stone (Guangxi, photo taken by the author).

The basin experience influence to the model of Feng-shui in the culture of Chinese agriculture

We can't be entirely sure that modern Chinese people are the direct descendants of Peking Man or Lantian Man. Nor can we confirm that modern Europeans don't have genes from Peking Man, or that the Chinese nation does not have the blood of Neanderthals. Therefore, a safe assumption is that primitive Chinese people's hunting and gathering experience in the typical habitations mentioned earlier wasn't enough to shape the unique character of the Chinese ideal Feng-shui model or the ideal landscape model. But from cross-cultural comparison we can see that there are some obvious differences between the Feng-shui model and the ideal landscape models of other cultures, such as European Christian culture. The characteristics of the Feng-shui model inevitably stand out. If we look at these characteristics from the ecological experience and the ecological adaptation mechanisms of the history of Chinese culture, including the formative period and the later developing period, we will find that it was the basin experience during these periods of Chinese cultivation culture that molded Chinese people's preference for certain landscape structures, thus forming the Feng-shui model. Of course, the Chinese people or the Chinese nation I mention here refer in a relative sense to a human group that has been influenced by the dominant Chinese culture.

5.1 Cross-cultural comparisons: A brief discussion of the strengthening characteristics of the Feng-shui model

Every culture provides the members of a cultural circle a kind of landscape cognizance model that is an operating system for the relationship between humans and the landscape (Kaplan and Kaplan, 1982). As discussed in chapter 1, Feng-shui is merely the expression and explanation of an ideal landscape, and the ideal Feng-shui model is a template for explaining, designing, and creating landscape. Therefore, in this sense, Feng-shui doesn't exist solely in Chinese culture, but also in every other cultures, only under different names. Some historical and archeological research shows that, in ancient Mesoamerican culture,, Feng-shui (which came to be called geomancy) was implemented in urban planning and

design. In Aztec tradition, every city's main axial line and
the layout of its religious buildings were strictly designed
according to geomancy in order to achieve harmony between
the structures and the movements of celestial bodies. And
in this culture, Feng-shui seemed extremely sensitive to
caves and mountains. The central point of the Aztec city
Teotihuacán was built on top of a cave and the whole city
surrounded other caves. The ends of its main axial line (15
25' from east to north), which lay across mountains, were
both the highest points of the mountain, and the Moon
Temple (Moon Pyramid) was situated on its northern end.
This structure copied the shape of the northern peak behind
it (Carrasco, 1982). There also is a similar sense of "Feng-
shui" in other ancient cultures (see Wheatly, 1971; Michell,
1975; Pennick, 1979).

*Figure 78   The ancient Aztec city Teotihuacán that is believed to be designed according to the Aztec
Geomancy (Photo by the author).*

But the ideal Feng-shui model of Chinese culture (in a
broader sense, the ideal landscape model) has its unique
character when compared with other cultures. And now we
are going to explore the characteristics of Chinese people's
ideal landscape model in comparison with European
Christian culture. For clarity of discussion, we are going to
divide the characteristics into the following sections:

5.1.1 "A box within a box"—an emphasis on the characteristic of shelter

Although in both ancient Chinese cities and European
Baroque cities the axial line was emphasized, in the latter
it was a visual passage or a perspective line that took the

building as the visual or focal point, while in Chinese cities the axial line was merely symbolic and didn't act as a visual corridor. Sitting in Taihe Hall in the Forbidden City, Emperor Kangxi certainly could not see anything beyond Taihe Gate. And unless he was carried up to the top of Jingshan Mountain, he would surely not be able to see the axial line that went right across the city from north to south. Even if he were on top of Jingshan Mountain, he could only see the golden tiles on the rooftops. But at almost the same time, Louis XIV could have appreciated the fountains and giant sculptures along the three-kilometer-long radial axial line from the windows of the dancing hall and dining hall at Versailles (figures 79, 80, 81 and 82).

Whether it's the geometric Forbidden City, a royal family's palace and naturalistic garden, a quadrangle for common people, a garden belonging to ancient literati, or a holy

Figure 79 The Forbidden City of Beijing (photo taken by the author).

Figure 80   Versailles in France (photo taken by the author).

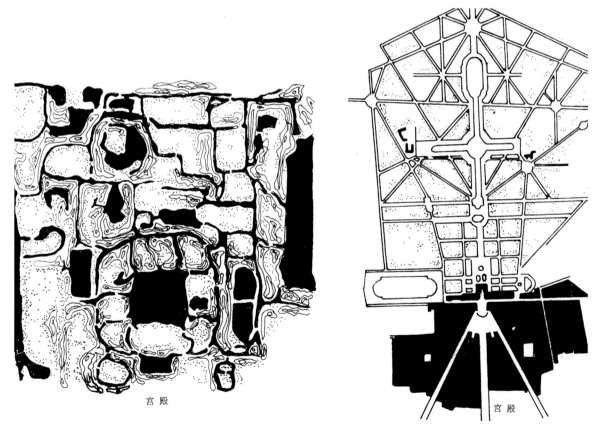

宮　殿

宮　殿

*Figure 81   The Grand Garden of YuanmingYuan – " a box in a box" and Versailles
in France in the same period of time – the occupation of the visual control point
(illustrated according to the topography).*

religious place, we can see from them all that the Chinese landscape model of habitation is still "a box within a box," with a strong preference for shelter structures. Whether they were artificial fences, screening walls, man-made hill or natural forests, they were all adapted to create enclosures and sheltering spaces (figure 79). As one of the wonders of the world and of the manmade Chinese landscape, the real meaning of the Great Wall does not lie in its ability to resist invasion from northwest nomadic tribes. As a matter of fact, the Great Wall never helped realize this goal or that of keeping the controlling power in the hands of the lords of the central land. On the contrary, from the Qin Dynasty to the end of the Ming Dynasty, each emperor's work on building the Great Wall only exhausted the workers, drained the treasury, and caused discontent among the people. In fact, it brought about the downfall of the kingdom. Therefore, both the Great Wall and other similar defensive systems (including the defensive system along the seashore built at the end of the Qing

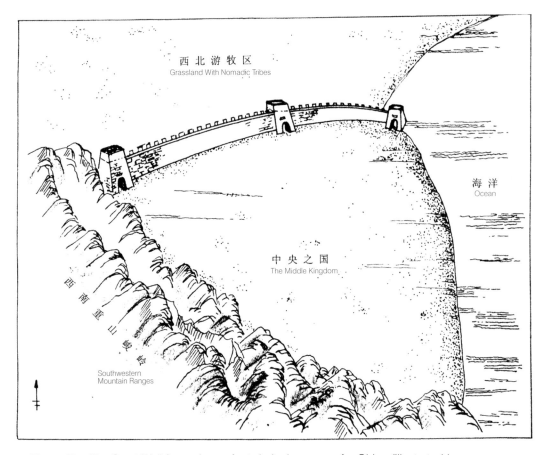

Figure 82 The Great Wall formed a perfect sheltering space for China (illustrated by the author).

Dynasty), only satisfied a psychological need. It did however express the strong preference for sheltering landscape structures that exists deep in Chinese culture (figure 85).

By comparison, European Christian culture expressed a strong preference for visual controlling and vantage points. And this preference manifested itself in the axial line (more precisely the visual corridor) that took the emperor's palace as its starting point (figures 80 and 81), through to the tower point of a church overlooking the whole town, and on to the castle on top of a mountain. Although a high position for a building location is considered best in the ideal Feng-shui models due to its relative independence and visual control of the bright hall, this kind of vantage point and visual controlling style will be limited in a city with many layers of fortresses. Even in ideal models such as Kunlun and Penglai, whose height and isolation are salient features, high mountains and islands are mainly useful as spatial separation. Obviously, landscape structures with vantage points and visual control are not emphasized in structures with multiple layers of fortresses, protective forests, or "gourd" shapes, which in fact express a strong preference for sheltering structures.

5.1.2 "A heavy fortress on all sides"—an emphasis on the characteristic of guarding territory

Structures that guard territory, which are related to the kinds of sheltering discussed above (enclosure and screening), are also emphasized in ideal Chinese Feng-shui models and ideal landscape models. This is shown in the emphasis on having a water mouth, and in the landscape structures of entrance-guarding and surrounding features. It is also evident in the attention given to gates in Chinese cities. A passage that is normally used to connect to the outside world and to explore and exploit what is beyond, has been endowed with a strong meaning of "barrier" in ideal Chinese landscape models, and is usually adorned with images of dangerous landscape features and scary dragons, tigers, or lions. The order in which an ancient Chinese city was built was to start with the wall, then build the gate, followed by the temple. It seemed that once these were built, the whole city was finished. This process was the opposite of temple- and city-building in India and Southeast Asia (Wheatley, 1971).

The Book of Songs tells us a story about building a city: "Bang bang bang! Let's build the wall, cut the wall straight, and we build walls everywhere ... then we set up the city gates; the gates are tall and strong. After setting up the front gate of the city, we build a temple and sacrifice the captives to gods." The process of building a city followed the order of wall, gate, temple here, and the magnificent city gate was highly praised. Even in the process of building a park in a modern Chinese city, the gate and the wall are always given priority and cost almost the whole amount budgeted for the first phase of the project. The emphasized ideal landscape characteristics discussed above are a manifestation of a preference for "hiding" and "defending" in Chinese culture. And the emphasis on vantage points and visual points in European culture are manifested by the action of "the paper tiger showing off," using attack as a means of defense. In the ideal landscape of Chinese culture, in which a favorite strategy is to "hide" and to "defend," this general characteristic is manifested: a sentimental attachment to and dependence on nature.

In the architecture of European culture, whether Byzantine, Gothic, classical, Baroque, or Rococo, there is a penchant for magnificence and the decoration of the building itself. By contrast, in Chinese culture, the building itself seems less important than the surrounding natural landscape. In an architectural culture spanning 5,000 years, what we see is a simple and nearly unchanging model from the straw shelters of the primitive people of Banpo, to Taihe Hall in the Forbidden City. Not much attention was paid to decorating the building, because the intent of its users was to "hide" the building (which was the embodiment of the person himself) in the natural landscape instead of exposing it. The painting *An Ancient Temple Hides in the Deep Mountain* tells of the mystery of an ancient temple hidden so well in the mountains that people could only guess of its existence through the human traces of a monk who came out to fetch water. In the Feng-shui models and other ideal landscape models discussed in the first chapter, human activities happened only within the "point" (the building spot) that was surrounded by a natural "dragon," i.e., hill or water. We can say that the Forbidden City stresses the supremacy of rulers. But Jingshan Mountain, which is on the axial line (running north) is better considered as a "supporting mountain" with some symbolic meaning more than a barrier for blocking the cold wind from the northwest. It faintly reveals the sentimental attachment and dependence on the natural landscape. In the André Le Nôtre styled imperial court in European, a mountain like this was usually located at the end of an axial line as a focal point and a contrasting view for the building instead of being used as a backing mountain. The Qu River in front of Taihe Gate, and the Golden Water River in front of Tian'an Gate, share the same meaning, which is to reflect a sentimental affection for and dependence on nature. But the same kind of body of water was used as a view in the visual axis of European imperial court design, and its purpose was visual rather than practical (figure 80). The sentimental attachment and dependence on mountains and water is even more vividly and thoroughly expressed in the Grand View Garden, theYuanmingyuan (figure 81).

As early as the Tang Dynasty, mountains and rivers had become an independent theme in Chinese landscape painting, and human characters and buildings appeared merely as decoration. In some paintings, there didn't appear to be any human figures, but a potentially "livable" landscape was constructed in the mountains and rivers, which were taken as objects to rely on. No matter how majestic and impressive the mountain is in the painting, its purpose is always to reveal an inner harmony that "purifies and eases the soul" (Daojian Pi, 1982). The painter's highest aesthetic goal was to convey his feelings and thoughts, evincing a strong sentimental affection and dependence on natural landscape. Meanwhile, in Europe, landscape painting did not appear as an independent undertaking until the seventeenth century, with the rise of the Dutch painting style. In addition to emerging more than a thousand years after Chinese landscape painting, it showed humans as the dominant feature, even in paintings of completely natural landscapes. In European landscape paintings, "even in front of a gentle and peaceful painting, you can still more or less sense a heart filled with desires" (Daojian Pi, 1982). This sort of natural craving and aggressive spirit is certainly very different from seeking a shelter in nature for a peaceful and private living space.

In short, the landscape dreams of Chinese people emphasize the functions of sheltering and guarding territory, and manifest a dependence on and sentimental attachment

Table 4   The comparison of the emphasized characteristics of ideal landscape models in both Chinese and European cultures.

emphasized characteristics of ideal landscape models in Chinese culture	The emphasized characteristics of ideal landscape models in European culture
1.The strategy of hiding; hide the human traces into the natural landscape	1.The strategy of showing off; emphasizes decoration and the position of the building
2. The strategy of defence; fills the space with strong guarding fortresses	2. The strategy of invasion; occupies the vantage point and the visual controlling point
3. Depends on nature	3. Overrides nature
4.With introspective "character"	4.With outgoing "character"

Figures 83–84   Two different strategies in taking a place in the landscape: the strategy of hiding or taking refuge that has been strengthened in the Chinese culture (A typical Chinese agricultural settlement in Wenshan County, Yunnan Province, photo by the author), vs. the strategy of prospect or attacking that has been strengthened in the European Christian culture illustrated by the ancient town of Orvieto in Italy (photo by the author).

to natural landscape in all areas. This is in sharp contrast to landscape dreams in European Christian culture (table 4). If such a dramatic difference exists between the Chinese ideal landscapes and those of the European counterparts, we must ask ourselves what other reasons have contributed to the formation of the Chinese ideal landscape beside the commonly shared biological genes based on primitive people's hunting and gathering experience? How important is the ecological experience of the Chinese culture for its development.

5.2 Guanzhong basin—an emphasis on the Feng-shui model in the period of cultured settlement

Like biological adaptation, cultural adaptation can also become a nation's hallmark through the copying and spreading of cultural genes. It doesn't matter whether these adaptations have a realistic utility or not. If we say that, due to biological heredity, primitive people's ecological experience of hunting and gathering formed a deep mental structure for a sense of good or bad fortune in Chinese landscape, then ecological experience during the settlement period built both landscape dreams and a deeper structure for sensing good or bad fortune through the means of cultural accumulation. Thereafter, through a continuous revising and emphasizing of the duplicating mechanism in biological and "cultural" genes, the ideal landscape model with Chinese cultural characteristics—the Feng-shui model—was formed.

The Zhou Dynasty (1056–256BC), which was established by the people of Jizhou and played an important role in linking past and present, thus setting a new course for later dynasties, was a settlement period in the development of Chinese national culture. It is acknowledged among historians that the civilization of the Zhou Dynasty affected social development deeply and extensively (Changwu Tian, 1990). The esteem for the etiquette of the Zhou period held by the culture of Confucianism and its idea of taking West Zhou society as the ideal, made Zhou Dynasty culture prominent in shaping Chinese culture. The post-figurative cultural characteristics of agricultural society brought about the etiquette system and behavior models of Zhou society, including the cognitive models of landscape, to be copied and spread through all sorts of classics, including *The Four Books* and *The Five Scriptures*. These resounded through many generations, becoming an outstanding feature of Chinese culture. The regulations of the Zhou Dynasty, especially concerning the royal palace design and city management, have a close relationship with the theme of this book. Some classics, such as *Government Guidance to Technicians and Craftsmen of Kingdom Qi, The Book of Chronological History by Zuo Qiuming, and The Book of Rites,* among others, were adopted by all the later dynasties in their architecture. From the Han Dynasty (202BC–220AD), the memorial buildings, such as the imperial temple, Sajik, bright hall, etc., were in large part built according to the documents and traditions handed down from the Zhou Dynasty (Dunzhen Guo, 1984).

We especially need to point out that the original model of a courtyard, which is one of the characteristics of Chinese architectural culture, was also formed during the early period of the West Zhou Dynasty (1046–771BC). From the "big house" of a community of clans in the Yangshao culture of the Banpo people, to the "family house of the late Xia Dynasty (2070–1600BC)" during the beginnings of slavery, to the Shang Dynasty's (1600–1046BC) style with a hall in front and rooms at the back, there was not an obvious change in our ancestors' building patterns until the West Zhou Dynasty, when architectural layout essentially changed (Hongxun Yang, 1987). A complete courtyard layout appeared. If we compare the main palace remnants from the early Shang Dynasty in Erlitou with the original courtyard in Fengchu from the Zhou Dynasty, we notice that in the original Zhou buildings, the middle and front halls were already separated, a screen wall appeared, and a courtyard replaced the original position of the main .hall. I believe that this leap essentially manifested an enhanced sense of sheltering and guarding territory among the Zhou people, which later developed into a hallmark of Chinese culture.

Most of *The Book of Changes*, which spans a long period of history, was formed throughout the period from the beginning of the Zhou Dynasty to the establishment of the West Zhou Dynasty (Kongjian Yu, 1990). From a historical point of view, *The Book of Changes* also reflected the natural, sociological, and ecological experience of the settlement age. As one

of the most influential and foundational books of scripture,
each word of which was taken literally, *The Book of Changes*
formed the basis from which the whole system of Feng-shui
theory originated (Kongjian Yu, 1990).

The explanation above is enough to prove that the ecological
experience and adaptation of Zhou culture can further reveal
the deep meaning of good and bad luck (sense of Feng-
shui) in the Chinese landscape. Most of the activities of
cultural settlement during the Zhou period took place in
the Guanzhong basin, which traced a central line across
Qishanand Chang'an City. This meant that the natural and
sociological ecological experience in the basin boosted the
development of a unique Chinese sense of good and bad
luck (Feng-shui) in landscape. It strengthened a preference
for sheltering and guarding structures of and an affection for
and dependence on nature in the ideal Chinese landscape.

5.2.1 Guanzhong basin—a bridge between biological and cultural genes

To the Zhou nation, which was going through a transitional
period of moving from a hunting society to a farming and
livestock breeding society around 3000 to 3500 years ago,
the ecologically satisfying habitations of primitive people still
held great attraction. Guanzhong Basin, which was where the
Zhou tribes lived, is located in the Wei River valley, with the
Qinling Mountain range to the south, a loess plateau to the
northwest, and the Taihang Mountain range to the east. It is
a long, deep, narrow basin. Compared with the surrounding
mountains and plateau, the relative altitude of the basin is
between 500 and 1,000 meters above sea level. It is 360
kilometers long, and at its narrowest, measuring from north
to south, is only a few hundred meters wide, with the central
area being about 30 kilometers wide. Many tributaries from
the surrounding mountains and plateau run into the basin
and thence into the Yellow River. This forms many water
mouths and valley corridors, which connect Hanzhong Basin,
southwest Shanxi Basin, the northwest nomadic area, and
the eastern great plain. The active center of the developing
and growing period of the Zhou nation was in the southwest
of the basin—Qishan Mountain at the southern edge was
its epicenter. This mountain resembled the "breast nipple"
type position and the land with "embryo" type site in the
bright hall of Feng-shui, which allowed the Zhou nation to

lean on Qinling Mountain and overlook the valley of the Wei River (figure 85). The entire landscape structure was similar to the satisfactory habitation pattern of primitive Chinese people. The only difference was that it was relatively large due to an increasing population and the agricultural and military activities of the whole nation. In fact, the valley of the Bahe River, where the Lantian People lived, was a fractal of Guanzhong Basin, situated at a corner of the big basin (figure 64).

It was no accident that the Zhou people chose this basin as their home. From their earliest habitation in Tai (in Gongwu County in Shaanxi), to Bin where they later moved (around the Bin County and Xunyi areas of Shaanxi), and on to Zhouyuan (around the Qishan and Xiefeng areas), the main centers of activity during the developing period of Zhou, and finally Feng and Gao (in Shanxi); the habitations of the Zhou people in the peak period of development were all places that were carefully selected. *The Book of Songs•Gongliu* vividly describes the historical story of Gongliu, who moved from Tai to Bin, selecting lands and founding his country: "Gongliu, an earnest person, inspected this place... climbed

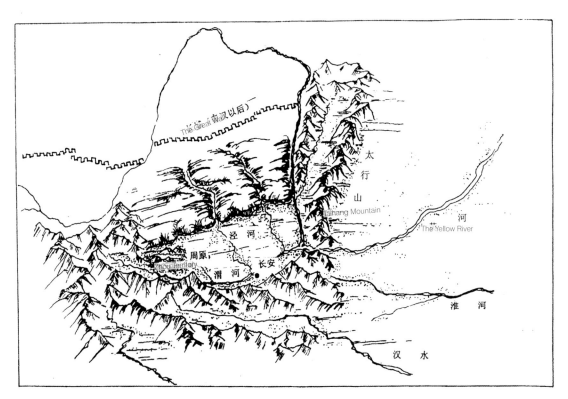

Figure 85 The diagram of the whole landscape structure of Guanzhong Basin (Kongjia Yu, 1990).

up the mountain and came down to the plain ... then came
to the bank of many rivers. Looking at the vast plain and
climbing the southern mountain, he then decided on the
place to build the capital city and the dwellings around the
city.... he inspected the direction of the mountain according
to the shadow of the sun and the rivers and springs on the
land." *The Book of Songs•Mian* also tells the story of the
king of Zhou, Taiwang, who moved to the district of Qi and
established his country: "Next morning, the honored man
Tanfu rode his horse along the river towards the west and
camped at the foot of Qi Mountain. Together with his wife
Jiangnu, he inspected the surrounding landscape."

Historians believe that King Taiwang's move to Qi signaled a
significant change and a leap forward in the history of Zhou's
development. Zhou society started to prosper at this turning
point (Changwu Tian, 1990). *The Book of Songs•Stories of
King Wen* also recorded King Wen moving to the district of
Feng, and King Wu moving to the district of Gao seeking
prosperity. From these stories, we can see that the ancestors
of many generations of Zhou were busy moving around
Guanzhong Basin in order to select living places, though we
don't know the specific criteria for their choices.

5.2.2 Guanzhong Basin—a cultivated territory with strategic advantages for shelter and guarding territory

A general shortage of resources and their uneven distribution
meant that areas with relatively concentrated resources that
were easy for tribes to guard made for ideal territory. In the
middle and upper reaches of the Yellow River, on the vast
loess plateau amid rolling mountains, the valley plain of the
Wei River could be called an oasis of the most concentrated
agricultural resources. Furthermore, this oasis, with its
numerous natural barriers, was easy to guard. In *The Poem
of the Two Capital Cities,* Ban Gu of the Donghan Dynasty
(25–220AD) described it thus: "There are Bao River and Xie
River on the right boundary with Long Mountain as barriers.
There are also big rivers like Jing and Wei. It has the most
abundant resources in the whole country, and the defensive
landscape is the most difficult to fathom in the whole world."

The advantage of sheltering and guarding territory was further strengthened after the Zhou people moved the capital city to the Zhouyuan plain. This plain (an elevated platform), which was the direct living environment of the people of Zhou, leaned on Qishan Mountain to the north and faced the Wei River to the south. There were the Qi and Qian rivers on both sides of it. The entire plain was about 70 kilometers long from east to west, and about 20 kilometers wide from north to south. This was a natural shelter in Guanzhong Basin for the tribe to maintain its survival and keep the strategic advantage of controlling the basin, even if the tribe had to retreat under great pressure in this guardable territory. From the point of view of the characteristics of landscape structure, there is no doubt that it was an ideal site for the capital, located high above the bright hall of a structure with mountain enclosures and with Xuanwu (black tortoise) to lean on. The adaptation to a territory with many layers of protection and guarding structures, as well as the cultural ecological experience of this kind of landscape, undoubtedly strengthened the Zhou people's preference for and dependence on landscapes with shelter and easy protection.

5.2.3 From "running away from danger" to "avoiding the northeast and turning to the southwest"—the strategic advantage of retreat

From the spatial distribution relationship between the Zhou and other tribes (figure 86), we can see that the aggressive nomadic tribes were on the northwest side, and the powerful kingdom of Shang and its tribes were on the northeast. Obviously, Zhou had enemies on three sides and had to survive in a difficult situation. While being an enemy with Shang, they had to repel attacks from the nomadic tribes. "To attack is not good for the relationship with [Shang], but good for resisting the invading tribes." This divinatory comment about "attacking" in *The Book of Changes* reflects Zhou's situation clearly. When they had a chance, the Zhou people also attacked one tribe with another tribe's power by taking the advantage of "being on the edge area." In *The Book of Changes*, the divinatory comment on "Weiji" said, "Rise up and attack the tribe of Guifang to assist the big Kingdom of Shang for three years." There were more than eighty divinatory comments about the wars between Zhou and other tribes in *The Book of Changes*, which effectively proved the significant role played by competition among the tribes regarding the development of the Zhou, who were always on the competing edge.

While under pressure from invasion and competition with strong tribes from three directions, Zhou found great peace in the nature of Qishan Mountain and the vast mountain range of Qinling to the south and southwest of the country. Living a life on the boundary of social cruelty and beautiful nature, the people of Zhou certainly cherished the beauty of nature and considered life in the mountains of the southern and southwestern areas to be the template for an ideal society. The divinatory comment on "Zhongfu" in *The Book of Changes* says, "The crane sings in the shade of the forest and the small crane is singing along. I have good wine and I would like to share with you." This reveals the longing of the people for a peaceful society, in harmony with the rest of the world. Therefore, comments about good or bad directions in *The Book of Changes* always considered the southwest (the mountain areas of Qishan and Qinling) to be good, and the northeast (the living area of the strong kingdom of Shang and other aggressive nomadic tribes) to be bad. For example,

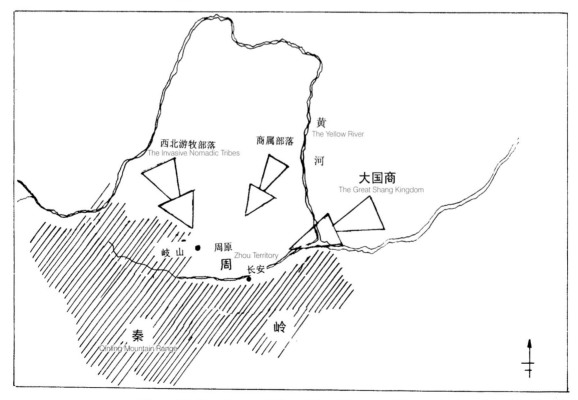

Figure 86   The diagram of the relationship among Zhou and other tribes (Kongjian Yu, 1990).

the divinatory comment in "Jian" says that "it is good to avoid the northeast and turn to the southwest and strengthen the relationship with the big country." And in the divinatory comment on "Chuan," it says, "turn to the southwest and it is easy to come and go. Good direction." The love of natural mountain life in the southwest, and a peaceful state of mind were further developed into the pursuit of flight and self-protection, which encouraged the strategies of "retreating" and "escaping" (see the divinatory comment on "flight" in T*he Book of Changes*). And these strategies, which were the essential secret of the Zhou people, finally helped them to conquer the territory of the other tribes after competing with them on the boundary. The strategies contained the "cultural genes" of depending on the natural landscape of shelter that also existed in Chinese people's sense of Feng-shui. Even the Zhou people's patterns of sensing good or bad directions— "turn to the southwest and avoid the northeast"—was to a great extent inherited and adapted by Feng-shui theory.

5.2.4 From "Chen" "Huan" (the divinatory comments) to "lucky forest"—the effects of disasters in Guanzhong Basin

At the edge of the loess plateau where the Zhou people started their activities in the early period, natural disasters such as floods and landslides occurred frequently due to serious water loss and soil erosion, regular earthquakes, and significant changes in elevation. Beside this, the valley of the Wei River was an earthquake zone and many strong earthquakes occurred there throughout history. Some divinatory comments, such as "Huan" (flood) and "Chen" (earthquake), in *The Changes of Zhou*, a book made of silk, vividly recorded the Zhou people's experience of these natural disasters (Qiubai Deng, 1987). Through this prolonged experience, the Zhou people gradually understood the natural ecological processes and ecological relationship between man and nature. They gained knowledge of forests, such as "it is beneficial to protect forests," "the overuse of forests will cause disasters," "to limit the use of forests will prevent disasters," and "the king should have knowledge about forests" (the divinatory comments about forests in *The Book of Changes*). All this knowledge revealed that the Zhou people not only noticed the direct practical functions of forests, but also realized the forest's ecological function in preventing water loss and soil erosion, and reducing the disasters of flood and drought. They therefore concluded that it was "good luck" to protect a forest, and "bad luck" to damage it. This ecological experience of agriculture directly affected the formation of good and bad senses of landscape, and encouraged the maturing process of an ecological sense (Kongjian Yu, 1990) and the dependence on a healthy natural ecosystem. But *The Book of Changes* only reflected the pattern of intuitive judgment of "phenomenon—good or bad," and did not provide any analysis about the causal relationship between the two things. This forced Feng-shui theory to find a new explanation system for itself after it took in the pattern of intuitive judgment. For example, Feng-shui theory considers a flourishing forest on top of a mountain to be a lucky sign. The explanation for this is that a forest gathers Qi.

We can see how the landscape characteristics, ecological experience, and cultural adaptation of Guanzhong Basin strengthened the Zhou people, and how they displayed the behaviors of taking shelter and guarding territory, showing a preference for the corresponding landscape structure of the entire Chinese nation.

The European experience was entirely different from the ecological experience of the main shaping period in Chinese culture. A key development zone of European culture was Crete in the Aegean Sea. And at almost the same time as the West Zhou Dynasty (800 to 510 BC), European culture went through its shaping period on the Greek Peninsula, on the islands in the Aegean, and in coastal areas. It was centered in the Aegean (Stavarianos, 1970), and later spread rapidly to the coastal areas of the Mediterranean. Compared with Guanzhong Basin, the ecological experience of primitive European people was different in at least the following respects:

First, the climate was totally different. The Aegean area is controlled by a Mediterranean climate that is rainy in winter and dry in summer. It was completely different from the monsoon climate of Guanzhong Basin. Considering the thermal radiation, summer was the most suitable season for growing crops, which means that primitive European people lacked a climate that was optimal for agriculture (figure 87).

But in Guanzhong Basin, the monsoon in summer brought abundant rain for crops during the growing season when thermal radiation was also sufficient, providing the best conditions for cultivation.

Second, since the primitive people of Aegean area lacked a productive wet river valley or basin landscape with rich resources like Guanzhong Basin, which was easy to guard, they didn't have a self-sufficient, natural sheltering place in which to live. The poor soil and scanty resources in the area made the guarding of habitations meaningless. Therefore, there was neither the soil nor the space to support a society with concentrated power, and the scarce resources could only maintain scattered small cities that were centered around

Figure 87　A sparse olive forest in the Mediterranean climate (Crete Island, photo taken by the author).

a castle on a vantage point. The castle itself became the gathering place for riches, replacing the low-yielding living place. It became an object that was worth guarding. And no doubt the people depended on and entrusted their emotions to the manmade castle, and not to the hidden natural landscape. What took the place of the Zhou people's affection and dependence on the natural landscape was primitive European people's confidence in their own strength. In a situation with no natural shelters to hide in or rely on, invasion and displays of strength became the best self-protection, and the corresponding strategy was to frighten other people and make them retreat by showing off power (instead of hiding). Therefore, castles usually took over vantage points and islands, taking control of a strategic circulating corridor in order to achieve the greatest advantage in strategic invasion and effectively show off their power (figures 88, 89, and 90).

A habitation structure that used vantage points and islands as a primitive people's direct living environment had an excellent ecological effect and was one of the structural characteristics of their satisfactory habitation. In European culture, the preference for this kind of structure was obviously strengthened, while it was clearly weakened in the ideal Chinese Feng-shui model.

In short, the main shaping period of European culture and the regional ecological experience there strengthened invasive behaviors and self-confidence, while relatively weakening the behaviors of seeking shelter and guarding territory, as well as trusting in nature. Christian culture is in essence expansive. It treated both people and nature in the same way. Ecological experience and cultural adaptation in early cultivating societies gradually caused differences between Chinese and European ideal landscape models. But these cross-cultural differences only appeared due to both cultures' emphasis on some common ideal landscape structures in human biological genes in different directions. Therefore, compared to this model, which surpasses biological genes, the cross-cultural differences in ideal landscape models happen at the secondary level.

Figure 88   The remains of Knoss Palace at Minos (Crete Island, 20000-1400 B.C.): controlling the thoroughfares within and without the island (photo taken by the author).

Figure 89   The remains of the ancient city of Phaistos in Minos (Crete Island, 1900-1400B.C.); built on the mountain and overlooking the Messara Plain on the island (photo taken by the author).

Figure 90   Acropolis, Athens, built in 500 B.C.; taking over the vantage point (photo taken by the author).

5.3 The basin experience in the process of cultural development: a reemphasis on the Feng-shui model

Chinese culture, after it basically gained its shape and orientation around the period of the West Zhou Dynasty (1046–771BC), started its continuous developing process. No matter how many dynasties passed or how many invasions by other tribes occurred, the development of Chinese cultivation culture never strayed from its inherent pattern. Its continuity and stability has been highly praised by historians and has never been equaled by any other culture. Over the course of more than three thousand years, the specific landscape model of "basin" continually accompanied the development of Chinese culture. The long period of ecological adaptation to "basins" further strengthened the characteristics of sheltering, guarding territory, and depending on nature in the Chinese Feng-shui model, causing it to diverge further from the European model.

Figure 91   A typical landscape with a village occupying a small basin in the Ancient Huizhou district, which is featured with numerous small fertile basins within a vast expansion of rolling hills. This district played as perfect refuge for Chinese who escaped from the great Central China plain whenever social turmoil or wars happened. Such a landscape is planned and designed for good feng-shui, with the settlement siting at the foothill, backed by the forested hill, with couple old Feng-shui trees as recognizable land mark, a Feng-shui-shui forest at the water mouth in front of the village, and an entrance corridor along a creek leading to outside. This landscape is exactly depicted in the Land of Peach Blossoms. (Xunjiansi, Wuyuan County, Jiangxi Province, photo by the author.)

5.3.1 The Guanzhong basin accompanies the maturing process of Chinese culture

From the West Zhou to the Sui (581–618AD) and Tang dynasties, over almost the entire period that shaped and matured Chinese

Figure 92   Taking place at the edge is good for Feng-shui, is actually an ecological prudent strategy to saving the fertile soils at the bottom of the basin.

culture, which experienced eleven emperors over nearly eleven hundred years, Guanzhong Basin was at the center of Chinese civilization and was the radiating source of Chinese culture. This period included the most influential dynasties in Chinese history, such as West Zhou, Qin (221–207BC), the first kingdom of Chinese feudal society), Han (the first climax of Chinese agricultural development), and Sui and Tang (the fully mature period of Chinese feudal culture). We can say that the ecological experience and adaptation of the Zhou people in Guanzhong Basin was sustained and strengthened, and that therefore the strengthening significance of the Guanzhong Basin experience on the Feng-shui model is self-evident.

5.3.2 The generality of using the basin in Chinese cultivated territory

Among various landforms in China, mountain areas comprise 33 percent and hills and basins 29 percent, while plains make up only 12 percent and are mainly located in the China's east and northeast regions, the middle and lower reaches of the Yangtse River, and in the Pearl River delta in the south. But these big plains were not suitable for habitations or cultivation at the beginning of agricultural civilization because they were almost all in an unsteady stage of flooding. Even on the north China plain, which was the earliest to be cultivated, the course of the Yellow River has changed again and again over the last two thousand years. As for the northeast plain and the Pearl River delta, before the Tang and Song dynasties they were mostly wilderness (compared to Han culture). Therefore, for long periods, agricultural resources in China were limited to patches of plains among valleys and basins. Limited resources and their uneven distribution combined with the basin's characteristic of being protectable, undoubtedly promoted a preference for landscapes with the strategic advantage of sheltering and guarding in Chinese cultivation culture.

Through the landscape and structure of the village of Yunrui on Qiqiao Mountain, we can gain more direct knowledge of the strong characteristics of sheltering, guarding, and depending on nature (figures 93 and 94). The residents of this village have survived by growing tea for generations. The village is located in a small basin on

Figure 93   The entire landscape of Yunrui village on Qiqiao Mountain (photo taken by the author).

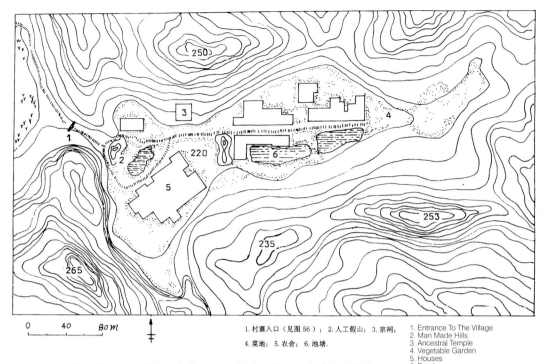

Figure 94   The diagram of Yunrui village on Qiqiao Mountain (Yu, 1992).

1. 村寨入口（见图 56）； 2. 人工假山； 3. 宗祠；
4. 菜地； 5. 农舍； 6. 池塘.

1. Entrance To The Village
2. Man Made Hills
3. Ancestral Temple
4. Vegetable Garden
5. Houses
6. Pond

top of Qiqiao Mountain, and is surrounded by hills of thick tall bamboo forests that were obviously the result of long-term protection. From site investigation, the traces of the effects of artificial strengthening on the surrounding hills can be seen. There was until recently only one winding passage to connect the basin with the outside world (another road was built recently in the northeast corner due to transportation needs). The small passage winds its way up the mountain, and there is an artificial hill and a gate to the village. Any intruder would only see the village after he walked around a pond behind the thickly wooded artificial hill.

5.3.3 The basin experience and the mechanism of ecological prudence

To a great extent, Feng-shui manifests respect, trust, and affection for natural processes and natural landscape and this is called ecological prudence. The formation of this mechanism of ecological prudence comes with two conditions: that this mechanism must bring a long-term benefit to the group, and that the group has the ability to protect the achievement of the mechanism (Gadgil, 1985). The several effects of a basin, which we will discuss below, are all helpful in satisfying these two conditions. In this way, the long period of basin experience advanced the development of the mechanism of ecological prudence in Chinese cultivation culture (Yu, 1991; Kongjian Yu, 1992).

(1) Basins were good at forming stable "eco-culture" regions. It was easy to use a basin to form an eco-culture region with a clear boundary (Dasmann, 1985), and the biogeographical region usually overlapped with the space of a cultural unit. The long-term relationship between the residents and the natural environment offered people a chance to get to know the process and structure of the basin's ecological system, and it was helpful for the people to learn the relationship between long-term and short-term benefits. This encouraged the development of a behavior of cultural ecological prudence.

(2) Basins were also good for the development of a sense of family and the ethic of continuing the family name. The size of a family and a certain social group needed to adapt to the size of the basin, since the future of the family or the entire group was totally dependent on this limited territory. Thus a strong sense of family was born. The story of how one's ancestors exploited and protected the homeland through hardship and wondrous feats was told to every family member by their elders, and this instilled a respect for one's forefathers that later developed into ancestor worship (figure 95). This was described as "a man of noble character traces his ancestors because he does not want to forget his origins. He wants to show respect and affection for them

Figure 95   Offering a sacrifice to the ancestors (photo taken by the author).

and work hard to return their love" (*The Book of Rites • Ethics*). Specifically, respect and worship for one's ancestors manifests as: First, every member of a family considered himself as one phase of family life, and his major function was to serve as a link between past and future generations in order to carry on the family. Therefore it is said, "three things were considered as disrespectful to parents, and the worst among them was not having offspring" (*Mencius • Liloushang*). Second, ancestral heritage was to be regarded as holy, and every man was responsible for keeping it as good as when it was received, to pass on to the next generation. "All those people who had property and blessings to protect and pass on to their descendants had ancestors who accumulated it for them. Therefore, children, you cannot forget about your ancestor for even one day." The morality of continuing the family name meant that you needed to consider the long-term benefit of the entire family while working for your own short-term gain. "Well dug by ancestors," "field handed down by ancestors," and "trees planted by ancestors," were an inheritance from the forefathers, and needed to be protected. If anyone dared to damage them, he would fall short of the ancestors' expectations and would lose face with his offspring. He would also be rejected by other people.

(3) Basins were good for forming social groups that excluded outsiders. There were four ways of occupying the space: personal occupation, community occupation, societal occupation, and free occupation (Brower, 1980). The proportions of the four ways of spatial occupation were quite different (figure 96) due to the variety of landscapes and ways of living. Line A is the most suitable one for describing the characteristic of spatial occupation of the relationship between basin landscape and lineage society. In a basin with limited

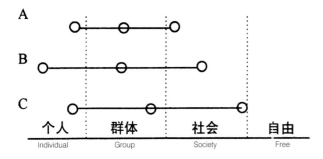

Figure 96 The proportional relationship of four kinds of spatial occupation in different landscapes and lifestyles (Brower, 1980).

size and a lineage society, personal spatial occupation was
also very limited, and nearly all of the space was commonly
occupied by the whole family or by all the members of a
close-knit society. There were few available social spaces,
and an intruder would usually raise the suspicion of the
whole village due to a strong need to repel strangers. Sharing
common space with family or the community made every
member feel responsible for protecting the land in order to
maintain his own benefit. Any individual's wasteful behavior
would be rebuked or severely punished by others in the group
so as to avoid "the tragedy of commons" (Hardin, 1968). The
repelling of outsiders and the ability to eliminate aberrant
behavior within the group proffered rewards for ecological
prudence to the whole community.

(4) Basins were also good at developing an indigenous,
self-sufficient economy. The isolating function of a basin
developed an indigenous lifestyle (Sach, 1980) that aimed
to satisfy the needs of the people instead of imitating other
people. The principle of the lifestyle was to be satisfied and
content (figure 97). The purpose of production was to provide
for the community instead of exchanging with other people.
The material and energy exchange of basins with the outside
world was very limited, and inner economic activities didn't

Figure 97   Being satisfied and content (photo taken by the author).

depend on the outside world much. Agricultural activities were directly restrained by the ecological mechanism within the basins, and thus adaptive behaviors, which included ecological prudent behavior, came into being. Experience has shown that a culture with exogenous consumption and a dependent economy means that the value standard of a different culture will be adopted to measure consumers' satisfaction and economic development levels. This usually causes damage to local resources (figure 98).

(5) Basin landscapes influenced the processes of other cultures. Due to spatial separation and the stability of the natural and social environment compared with the agricultures of other landforms, basin agriculture had a more concentrated population that was usually nearly at the limit of the carrying capacity of the ecosystem. Some people believed that the pressure of population saturation was helpful in advancing the development of cultural ecological-prudent behavior (Gadgil, 1985). In long-term isolation, the development of basin technologies stagnated for a long period of time, and people became more dependent on the power of regenerating traditional resources for further production (figure 99) in order to obtain more benefit from ecological prudent behavior.

Figure 98 The promotion ads a normal American household receives everyday: an exogenous demand-oriented society wastes resources (photo taken by the author in his Cambridge, MA home, 1995).

*Figure 99   The long-term low productive level
was helpful for the development of the ecological
restraint mechanisms (Taihang Mountain in Henan,
photo taken by the author).*

*Figure 100   The experience of disasters; drought
and limited water resources promoted the
development of ecological restraint mechanisms
(Liannan, Guangdong, photo taken by the author).*

On the other hand, rapidly developing technology caused people to constantly exploit new resources in order to move away from dependency on a specific resource, which wasn't conducive to ecological prudence.

(6) Basins experienced frequent natural disasters (figure 100). Compared with the large plains, basin landscapes had an obvious heterogeneity and complexity. Every basin had its own relatively independent ecological system, and disasters caused by the landscape of individual basins usually occurred within small areas. The effects on the entire landscape occurred gradually and with warning. The characteristics of a basin (such as the sharp contrasts in landforms that cause landslide, storm water from the surrounding hills that causes flood, etc.) determined the high frequency and intensity of disasters within a certain range. From the viewpoint of adaptation and systematic evolution, this was good for the advancement of cultural mechanisms of ecological prudence. On the other hand, on large plains (such as in Mesopotamia), relatively even ecological systems lacked variety, levels, and complexity. The ecological factors of agriculture in those areas were fairly unanimous, and therefore disasters caused by damage to the ecological balance were destructive and sudden.

Hence we can see that the basin experience in Chinese agriculture clearly encouraged the development of ecological prudence. Yet I must point out that ecological prudent behavior doesn't appear solely in the agricultural practices of Chinese basins. Many other cultures achieved the prudent usage and protection of certain kinds of resources through totemism, taboos, and religious customs, such as in India where there are many kinds of plants and animals strictly protected by religion. This prudent behavior is thought to have originated during the age of hunting and gathering (Gadil, 1985). Even Christian culture, which was considered to be nature-damaging, did not lack a tradition of loving nature and protecting animals (Vroom, 1985; FAO 1985). What I want to emphasize here is that, due to its unique basin experience, Chinese agriculture has distinguishing features that manifest mainly in its prudent behavior, and that this wasn't simply because of the need for the sustainable use of certain resources. Instead, its purpose was to continually use and protect the entire producing and living environment of agriculture. Feng-shui theory, as the interpretation and operating system of the Chinese people and their relation to nature and an ideal landscape, effectively reveals the ecological prudent mechanism of Chinese agricultural practice (Yu, 1994), and also forms the characteristics of depending on the whole natural environment affectionately while protecting the natural landscape.

5.3.4 The Unstable Great Plain and the model of the "Land of Peach Blossoms"

In the early years of development of the Great Plain of North China, there were constant wars that often caused that area to become unlivable. The residents there were either killed or forced to flee. In other words, it was hard to form a long-term, stable adaptive mechanism between the residents on the great plain and their habitat. On the contrary, the small basins in the Yangtze River area and the hilly land and small basins to its south were often peaceful, and became natural shelters for refugees. This happened frequently during the time of the Wei (21–3266AD) and Jin (266–420AD) dynasties when large number of Han people escaped to the south from the wars in the north. The "Land of Peach Blossoms" that Tao Yuanming imagined reflected this mentality of escaping into the mountains in search for peaceful habitats. In fact, the vast hilly land to the south of the Yangtze River had always been a refuge for expelled royal family members and the residents of the North China Plain, escaping from the wars among the big kingdoms during the Zhou dynasty or during invasion from outsiders (the nomadic tribes). That was not only a spreading process of Chinese culture but also a strengthening process of adaptation to basins, which made the Chinese people design their social dream of peace and harmony in a natural hilly basin that could be both protective and easy to defend. This ideal basin model was also the ideal Feng-shui model.

If we note that the Chinese basin experience, which occurred during the developmental stages of agriculture, reflected the continuity and strengthened form of the Guanzhong Basin experience and adaptation during its formative period, we can see that European culture also strengthened its ecological experience and adaptation along the Aegean Sea and its islands while spreading to the coastal areas of the Mediterranean and the vast areas of Europe. It was the different landscape and ecological experiences of these two cultures during formative periods that reinforced structural characteristics of ideal models of habitat in human biological genes, manifesting the differences and individual characteristics of ideal landscape models in both Chinese and European cultures.

The interpretation system of Feng-shui concerning the sense of fortune in landscape

As I stated at the beginning of this book, I have no intention of engaging in a deep discussion of the interpretation of Feng-shui theory and method themselves. There have been many books about it both in China and overseas (see the literature summary at the beginning of this book). I insert a chapter here simply for expressing my own opinion and summarizing the structure of this book.

The discussions in each chapter are meant to clarify the meaning of Feng-shui (the senses of good or bad landscape), to a large extent decided by human thought formed during the process of evolution and affected by the natural and social ecological experience of national culture during its formative period. These two influential factors together make up the deep meaning of Feng-shui. Primitive people's ideal habitat forged the original pattern for an ideal Feng-shui model. Moreover, the basin experience in Chinese agriculture during its early development strengthened some structural features of this original pattern. In this way, the sense of good or bad landscapes came into being.

Here I emphasize that it is Feng-shui theory that set up the interpretive systems regarding the sense of fortune in landscapes. These systems have three layers: the philosophical system of Huashi (start), Huaji (process), and Huacheng (achievement); the technological system of discerning Qi, which only a few experts have mastered; and the superstitious interpretive system that is accepted by the common people. These three interpretive systems form the surface structure of Chinese Feng-shui's meaning (Kongjian Yu, 1990) (figure 101). But the superficial explanations don't directly reflect the practical utility and functionality of landscape with a sense of fortune, and therefore Feng-shui theory and Feng-shui reading become more mysterious and illusory.

The first books about Feng-shui were written by Huang Shi (at the end of the Qin and beginning of the Han Dynasty), continued by Pu Guo (of the Jin Dynasty), and brought to a peak of popularity by Yang Junsong (of the Tang Dynasty). After that, many fake books appeared pretending to be the work of experts (such as *The Authentic Theory of Land* by Guo

Jiang). Although there is no consensus about the authenticity of Huang Shi's *Qingnang Scripture* and Guo Pu's *The Book of Burial*, the contribution of these two books to Feng-shui theory has been acknowledged. They basically established the philosophical and theoretical system under ancient Chinese philosophy. Feng-shui masters who came after Guo Pu added technical explanations to the theory and gradually made Feng-shui more mysterious and harder to understand. The discussion about Feng-shui theory here will be based mainly on the acknowledged classics of Feng-shui.

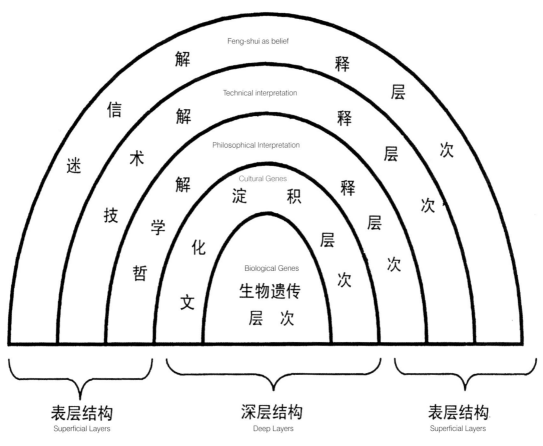

Figure 101   The deep structure and superficial structure of the meaning of Feng-shui (Kongjian Yu, 1990).

6.1 The philosophical interpretive system

In relation to the theory of ontology, although Chinese philosophy includes "Qiism," "Rationalism," and "Spiritualism" (Dainian Zhang, 1982), Qiism is the basic assumption that Qi is the originating substance of the world (meaning air or breath), existing yet surpassing all material form, from which the theoretical system of heaven, earth, life, and humankind in unity was established. This philosophy is certainly the specific "scientific" premise of Feng-shui, whose ultimate purpose is to pursue harmony between humans and nature. Through the logic of Huashi, Huaji, and Huacheng, Feng-shui theory transformed "Qi," the philosophical concept, into a specific operable system (figure 102).

Huashi believes that everything in the universe starts with Yin and Yang, and the reality of Qi is a great shapeless void that is filled with the Qi of Yin and Yang between heaven and earth. "The Qi gathers and scatters and changes into different forms," and "the hovering airs interact with each other and form into human beings and all other kinds of things; the one that recycles endlessly between Yin and Yang can establish itself between heaven and earth" (from Chapter *Taihe of Correction of Ignorance* by Zai Zhang). This is the basic ontological theory that believes that heaven, earth, humankind, and life can be in unity.

Huaji means that Qi, which has neither form nor weight, is not intangible. "When Qi gathers, it forms signs in heaven and shapes on earth." "There are five stars in heaven and five factors on earth; the heavens are formed by stars, and the earth is lined with mountains and rivers" (from *Qingnang Scripture*). Besides the everlasting bodies, Qi also has perceivable forms such as wind, rain, frost, snow, etc., what *The Book of Burial* describes by saying "the Qi of Yin and Yang moves as wind, rises as clouds, rolls as thunder, and descends as rain." The Qi of Yin and Yang not only has rules of change and movement in three-dimensional space, but also has a perceptible moving form in the dimension of time. Feng-shui theory adopted the movement relationship between the changes of day and night and seasons and Qi in Chinese philosophy, which is "day and night is a break in heaven; winter and summer is a day and night in heaven;

the Qi changes at the time of spring and autumn, just like a person who falls asleep and then wakes up" (by Zai Zhang, from Chapter *Taihe in Correction of Ignorance*). One of the most important features of Chinese philosophy is the unity of substance and human spirit (or mind) in Qi: "Whether birds or fish, animals or plants, clever ones or foolish ones, good or evil, all are attached to Qi ...any evil sound (music) will have evil Qi come to respond to it and produces evil signs and forms a troublesome environment; but a good sound will have good Qi come to respond to it and produces good signs and forms a smooth environment" (*Commentary on Correction of Ignorance* by Fuzhi Wang). Feng-shui theory inherited and developed this idea. In *The Book of Burial,* any burial that does not follow the morals of humanity or the rules of heaven is considered a "bad luck burial." "From the wrong order of Yin and Yang, wrong hour of burial, wrong way of showing off riches, wrong atmosphere, wrong relationship with people to wrong signs at the funeral, the degree of bad luck is considered to worsen." Therefore, the movement stage of Qi becomes a multivariable function:

$$Qi = F(c.l.o..m..o.t.h)$$

In the above equation, c =Celestial phenomena l =landform; o= orientation; m =meteorological signs; t = time; h = human spirit or mind; F stands for a certain kind of functional relationship. This equation has a solution: the living Qi brings the Yin and Yang and the five elements among all the variables into "Chonghe" (mutual harmony). Thus, the matching relationship and the restrictions among the five elements of Yin and Yang have been introduced as the principle of judgment (table 5, figure 102).

Huacheng stipulates that observation of the signs of sky and land, and judgments about seasons and directions were all based on the movement regulations of Qi, meaning "arranging things according to signs and divinatory comments, judging the fortune by the patterns of hour, prophesying the future according to the pattern of Qi, understanding geographic functions and making them benefit the people, and finally achieving completion following the changes" (*Qingnang Scripture*). When Yin and Yang are in mutual harmony, living Qi will be gained, blessings and prosperity will last forever, and everything else will come into being. By this time, the basic

Table 5   The matching relationship among the main variables with the five elements.

five elements	wood	fire	earth	gold	water
five stars	Sui (Jupiter)	Yinghuo (Mars)	Zhen (Saturn)	Taibai (Venus)	Chen (Mercury)
five directions	east	south	middle	west	north
seasons	spring	summer	midsummer	autumn	winter
morals	kindness	manners	faith	rightousness	wisdom
colours	green	red	yellow	white	black

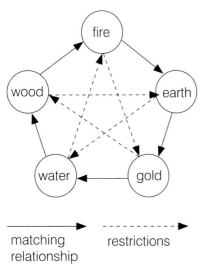

matching relationship

restrictions

Figure 102   The matching relationship and restrictions among the five elements of Yin and Yang.

technologies of Feng-shui were established, and the theory that "Qi scatters when wind blows and stops when it comes next to water" was suggested, producing the ideal Feng-shui landscape model of "hiding away from wind and being close to water."

Ancestor worship is one of the important characteristics of Chinese religious culture. To arrange everything for the deceased ones as if they were still alive is the main purpose of burial regulations in China. In the Chinese culture of ancestor worship, people believe that the ghosts of the dead and the ghost world are not any different from the real world, and are still made up of the Qi of Yin and Yang that exists between heaven and earth and can communicate with living ones through the senses (figure 103). Therefore, although in Feng-shui there are both houses of Yin (for the dead) and houses of Yang (for the living), they are basically not much different. The biggest mystery in Feng-shui theory, which believes that the burial of ancestors decides whether their offspring receive blessings or bad luck, also originated from this belief. "The Qi of the living person gathers and forms bones. After his death, the bones are the only thing left, and the people who buried him will take his Qi back and store it in their bones, and the Yin (the dead) will affect the living ones (from *The Book of Burial*)." Since every person receives his body from his parents and inherits the same Qi and blood system, therefore, when the living Qi of the parents' bones returns, they will naturally "sense it and receive the blessings from the deceased." So, to choose the right burial site for their parents is just as important as selecting the right site for building a house, the purpose for both being to "take the living Qi" and "receive everlasting blessings and prosperity" (figure 103).

The philosophical logic of Feng-shui developed from Chinese philosophy. Although it includes a complete theoretical system, it still lacks a basis in truth. The idea that the Feng-shui of the ancestors' burial can decide the offspring's fortune based on a belief that "the deceased can bless the offspring through the mutual sense of Qi"; deciding the relationship among the variables by the matching and restricting of the five elements; and taking the theory of "wind scatters Qi and water stops Qi" as the basic judgment of good or bad Feng-shui—these behaviors are obvious nonsense and are not based in fact. Therefore, Feng-shui theory did not produce the ideal pattern (landscape pattern) of the Chinese people. On the contrary, it was the ideal landscape pattern in the depth of the Chinese mind and culture that started the exploitation of Feng-shui dreams in Feng-shui theory and further established a whole interpretive system based on the Chinese philosophy

Figure 103   *The circulation of the living Qi of Feng-shui.*

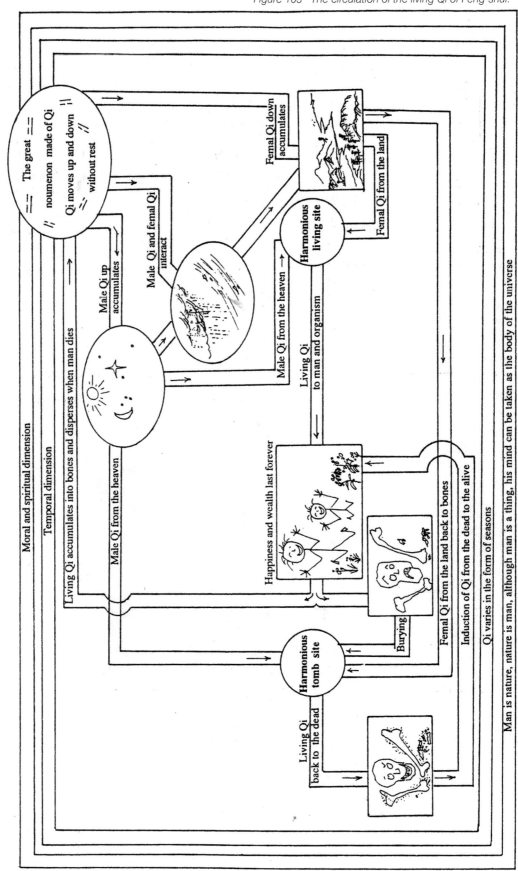

of Qi, though a systematic false interpretation. In this sense, Feng-shui theory itself doesn't have much meaning, but the in-depth meaning of its landscape dreams are worthy of our attention and are the starting point for this book.

6.2 The technical and "common believers" interpretive systems

Under the philosophical interpretive system, Feng-shui theory introduced a technical system of measurement, which took compass reading as a central skill. It made Feng-shui reading a very complicated technology and became a way for some people to make a living. Yet it is obviously difficult for the common Chinese people to understand the profound philosophy of Qi and to adopt the technology of Feng-shui, such as complicated compass reading. Therefore, the folk Feng-shui practitioner had to simplify the theory and make it easy for normal people to accept. And this could only work with the help of an original folk belief in ghosts, which I call common people's belief, to interpret Feng-shui theory and its technology. This has added a strong overlay of superstition to Feng-shui theory.

Conclusion

At the moment, most discussions of "Feng-shui theory," both in China and overseas, relate to the superficial structure of Feng-shui meaning. Therefore, some people believe it's superstitious, while others think it's scientific. In fact, just as we discussed above, Feng-shui theory doesn't explain the essence of the relationship between "landscape phenomenon and a sense of fortune"; instead it offers systematic interpretation detached from its deep meanings. Thus, whether we take this interpretive system as superstition or science, it doesn't help with the research of the relationship between landscape and fortune, which Feng-shui theory wants to explain. If we could further explore the history of the inception and development of the Chinese sense of fortune in landscape, analyze the deep meaning of the ideal Feng-shui model, and discover the rules for a solid relationship between humans and landscape, it would be beneficial for planning and designing landscape and for studying the relationship between man and nature. It would also benefit research into traditional culture, which not only refers to the study of Feng-shui theory, but also to the study of other cultural heritages, which would be carried on to a higher level.

Science or superstition? Amitabha! Feng-shui is only a cultural phenomenon. Why do we have to praise it or despise it? Its real meaning lies in the landscape dreams it reflects, which are a pattern of biological and cultural genes.

References

Bibliography of Publications in English

Alcock, J. *Animal Behavior: An Evolutionary Approach*. 3rd ed. Sunderland, MA: Sinauer Associates, 1984.

Appleton, J. *The Experience of Landscape*. Chichester, UK: John Wiley, 1975.

Bennett, S. J. "Patterns of the Sky and Earth: the Chinese Science of Applied Cosmology." *Chinese Science*, 3. University of Pennsylvania, 1978.

Boerschmann, E. *Picturesque China, Architecture and Landscape*, trans. L. Hamilton, based on travels in China, 1909.

Brower, S. N. "Territory in Urban Setting." *Human Behavior and Environment: Advances in Theory and Research* 4 (1980): 179-207.

Carrasco, D. *Quetzalcoatl and the Irony of Empire*. Chicago: University of Chicago Press, 1982.

Corner, J. "Most Important Questions." *Landscape Journal* 11, no. 2 (1992): 163-64.

Cronon, W. *Changes in the Land: Indians, Colonists and the Ecology of New England*. New York: Hill and Wan, 1984.

Dasmann, P. F. "Achieving the Sustainable Use of Species and Ecosystems." *Landscape Planning* 12 (1985): 211-19.

De Groot, J. J. M. *The Religious System of China*. Vol. 3, bk. 1, pt III, Ch. XII, 935-1056. Brill Leiden, 1897. Also reprinted as: de Groot, J. J. M. *Chinese Geomancy*. In: Walters, W. (ed.). Shaftesbury: Element Books.

Dukes, E. J. "*Feng-shui*." *Encyclopedia of Religion and Ethics* 5 (1914): 833-35.

Edkins, J. "*Feng-shui*." *Chinese Recorder and Missionary Journal*. Foochow, (March 1872): 274-77, and "On the Chinese Geomancy." *Recorder and Missionary Journal*, (April 1872): 291-98.

Eitel, E. J. *Feng-shui*. Kingston Press, 1873.

FAO. "Tree Growing by Rural People." *Forestry Paper* 64 (1985). Rome: Food and Agriculture Organization of the United Nations.

Feuchtwang, S. *An Anthropological Analysis of Chinese Geomancy*. Vientane, Laos: Vithagna, 1974.

Forman, R. T. T. and M. Godron. *Landscape Ecology*. John Wiley & Sons, 1986.

Freedman, M. "*Geomancy and Ancestor Worship*." *Chinese Lineage and Society: Fukien and Kwangtung*. London: Athlone Press (1966): 118-54.

Freedman, M. "Geomancy." *Proceedings of the Royal Anthropological Institute of Great Britain and Ireland, London, 1968* (1969): 5-15.

Gadgil, M. "Cultural Evolution of Ecological Prudence." *Landscape Planning* 12 (1985): 285-99.

Geist, V. *Life Strategies, Human Evolution, Environmental Design: Toward a Biological Theory of Health*. New York: Springer-Verlag, 1978.

Hardin, G. "The Tragedy of the Commons." *Science* 162 (1968): 1234-48.

Henry, B. C. *The Cross and the Dragon: Light in the Broad East*. New York: Anson D. F. Randolph and Co., 1885.

Hull, R. B. and G. B. Revell. "Cross-cultural Comparison of Landscape Scenic Beauty Evaluations: A Case Study in Bali." *J. of Environmental Psychology* 9 (1989): 177-91.

Johnson, S. *Oriental Religions and Their Relationship to Universal Religion: China*. Cambridge: John Wilson & Sons, 1881.

Kaplan, S. and R. Kaplan. *Cognition and Environment: Functioning in an Uncertain World*. New York: Praeger, 1982.

Knapp, R. G. *China's Traditional Rural Architecture: A Cultural Geography of Common House*. Honolulu: University of Hawaii Press, 1986.

Knapp, R. G. *China's Vernacular Architecture: House Form and Culture*. Honolulu: University of Hawaii Press, 1989.

Knapp, R. G. *Chinese Landscapes: The Village as Place*. Honolulu: University of Hawaii Press, 1992.

Lai, C-Y. "A *Feng-shui* Model as a Location Index." *Annals of the Association of American Geographers* 64, no. 4.

Lip, E. *Chinese Geomancy*. Singapore: Times Books International, 1979.

Lip, E. *Feng-shui for the Home*. Singapore: Times Books International, 1987.

Marcel, G. *The Religion of the Chinese People*, trans. and ed. M. Freedman. New York: Harper & Row, 1975. First published in French 1922.

March, A. L. "An Appreciation of Chinese Geomancy." *Journal of Asian Studies* 26 (Feb. 1968): 253-67.

Marsh, G. P. *Man and Nature*. Cambridge, MA: The Belknap Press of Harvard University Press, 1965.

McHarg, I. L. *Design with Nature*. Garden City, NY: The Natural History Press, 1969.

McHarg, I. L. "Human Ecological Planning at Pennsylvania." *Landscape Planning* 8, no. 2 (1981): 109-20.

Michell, J. Foreword to second ed. of *Feng-shui*. In: Eitel, E. J. *Feng-shui*. Kingston Press, 1973.

Michell, J. *The Earth Spirit*. New York: Thames and Hudson, 1975.

Morse, D. H. *Behavioural Mechanisms in Ecology*. Cambridge: Harvard University Press, 1980.

Naveh, Z. and A. S. Lieberman. *Landscape Ecology: Theory and Application*. New York: Springer-Verlag, 1984.

Naveh, Z. "Some Remarks on Recent Developments in Landscape Ecology as a Transdisciplinary Ecological and Geographical Science." *Landscape Ecology* 5, no. 2 (1991): 65-73.

Needham, J. *Science and Civilization in China* 4 (1962), *Physics and Physical Technology*. Cambridge University Press, 239-45.

Needham, J. *Science and Civilization in China* 2 (1956), *History of Scientific Thought*. Cambridge University Press, 359-63.

Needham, J. *Science and Civilization in China* 2 (1980), *History of Scientific Thought*. The Syndics of the Cambridge University Press.

Nemeth, D. J. *The Architecture of Ideology: Neo-Confucian Imprinting on Cheju Island, Korea*. University of California Press, 1987.

Partridge, L. "Habitat selection." In *Behavioural Ecology: An Evolutionary Approach*, ed. J R. Krebs and N. B. Davies, 351-76. Blackwell Scientific Publications, 1978.

Pennick, N. *The Ancient Science of Geomancy*. London: Thames and Hudson , 1979.

Rossbach, S. *Feng-shui: The Chinese Art of Placement*. E. P. Dutton, 1983.

Sach, I. "Cultural Ecology and Development." In *Human Behavior and Environment: Advances in Theory and Research*, ed. I. Altman et al. Vo1. 4: 319-43. New York: Plenum Press, 1980.

Schlegel, G. *Critique on De Groot (1897) the Religious System of China*. T'oung Pao, Series 1, Vol. 9 (1898): 65-78.

Simonds, J. O. *Landscape Architecture: A Manual of Site Planning and Design*. McGraw Hill, 1983.

Skinner, S. *The Living Earth Manual of Feng-shui*. London: Routledge & Kegan Paul, 1982.

Stavrianos, L. S. *The World to 1500: A Global History*. Englewood Cliffs, NJ: Prentice-Hall, 1970.

Vroom, M. J. "Religion and Environmental Attitudes: Cause and Effects?" *Landscape Planning* 12 (1985): 311-12.

Wheatley, P. *The Pivot of the Four Quarters*. Edinburgh University Press, 1971.

Xu, P. "*Feng-shui*: A Model for Landscape Analysis." Harvard Graduate School of Design, Thesis, 1990.

Yang, C. K. *Religion in Chinese Society*. Berkeley and Los Angeles: University of California Press, 1967.

Yates, M. "Ancestral Worship and *Feng-shui*." *Chinese Recorder and Missionary Journal* 1, 1868.

Yu, K-J. "Experience of Basin Landscapes in Chinese Agriculture Has Led to Ecologically Prudent Engineering." In *Human Responsibility and Global Change*, eds. Hansson, L. O. and B. Jungen. Proceedings of the International Conference on Human Ecology. Sweden: University of Gothenburg, 1992.

Yu, K-J. "Infinity in a Bottle Gourd: Understanding the Chinese Garden." *Arnoldia* (Spring 1993): 1-7.

Yu, K-J. "Landscape into Places: Feng-shui Model of Place Making and Some Cross-cultural Comparison." In *History and Culture*, ed. Clark, J. D.: 320-40. Mississippi State University, 1994.

Yu, K-J. "Cultural Variations in Landscape Preference: Comparisons among Chinese Sub-groups and Western Design Experts." *Landscape and Urban Planning* 32 (1995): 107-26

Bibliography of Chinese Publications

Deng, Q-B. *Commentary on The Silk Book of Zhouyi*. Hunan People's Press, 1987.

Deng, W-C. *The History of Chinese Painting*. Shanghai Books and Painting Press, 1983.

Feng, J-K. *The Site and Feng-shui of the Royal Tomb of the Qing Dynasty*, additional vol., Tianjin University Sinica, 1989.

Gu, Y-W. (Qing Dynasty), *Changing Landscape*. Beijing Classics Press, 1980.

He, X-X. *Exploring Feng-shui. Southeast* University Press, 1990.

Jia, L-P and Weiwen Huang. *The Excavation of Zhoukoudian*. Tianjin Science Press, 1984.

Liu, D-Z. *A Chinese History of Ancient Architecture*, 2nd ed. Chinese Architecture Press, 1984.

Liu, Y-H. *A New Exploration of the Beginning of Chinese Civilization: Daoism and the Cosmology of the Yi Minority*. Yunnan People's Press, 1985.

Lu, M-J. *The Research of the Relationship Between Ancient "Feng-shui Theory" and the Development of Cities: Thoughts of Planners across Centuries,* ed. Bao Shixing. Architecture and Industry Press, 1990.

Luo, Z-W. *Chinese Ancient Pagodas*. Chinese Youth Press, 1985.

Pan, J-Y. *Human Ecology*. Fudan University Press, 1988.

Pan, T-S. *History of Chinese Painting*. Shanghai People's Fine Arts Press, 1983.

Pi, D-J. *Observation on the National Aesthetic Sense from the Development of Chinese Landscape Painting, Study on Chinese Painting*, 2nd ed. People's Fine Arts Press, 1982.

Qi, H, and W. Fan. *The Feng-shui Pattern of the Ancient City of Langzhong*, additional vol. Tianjin University Sinica, 1989.

Tian, C-W., ed. *The Estimate of the Social Developing Stage at the End of the Shang Dynasty, The Civilization of China*, Beijing University Press, 1990.

Tian, C-W. *The Civilization of China* vol. 2, Beijing University Press, 1990.

Wang, Q-H. *The Feng-shui Research of the Qing Royal Tombs*. additional vol. Tianjin University Sinica, 1980.

Wang, Y-D. *Mysterious Feng-shui*. Guangxi People's Press, 1990.

Wen, J., trans. *Feng-shui Theory and Chinese Cities*, additional vol. Tianjin University Sinica, 1998.

Wu, S-M. *Change in Chinese Landscape Painting*. Shanxi People's Publishing House, 1988.

Wu, L-F. *Research of the Theory of Chinese Painting*. Beijing University Press, 1983.

Yang, H-X. *A Collection of Theses about Architectural Archaelogy*. Cultural Relic Publishing House, 1987.

Yu, X-X et al. *"Chinese Feng-shui Thought and Site Selection for Cities."* Global Geography Magazine (May 1990): 93-107.

Yu, K-J. *"The Main Schools and Methods of Landscape Resource Estimation, Young Landscape Designers (corpus)."* Intelligence Information of Urban Design (1988): 31-41.

Yu, K-J. *"An Estimation of the Quality of Natural Landscape*: BIB-LCJ *Aesthetic Evaluation Measurements."* Beijing Forestry University Sinica 10, no. 2 (1988a): 1-11.

Yu, K-J. *"On the School of Cognition's Estimation of Landscape Aesthetic Quality."* Chinese Garden 1 (1988b): 16-19.

Yu, K-J. *"An Exploration of the Deep Meaning of Feng-shui Patterns, an Exploration of Nature"* 9, no. 1, (1990).

Yu, K-J. *"A Study of the Edge Effect of the Ecological System from the Viewpoint of Yi Scripture."* Yi Scripture and Modern Natural Science, eds. D-Y Xu et al. Chinese Social Science Publishing House (1990a).

Yu, K-J. *"The Ideal Environment Pattern and a View of the Ecological History of the Chinese People."* Beijing Forestry University Sinica 12, no. 1 (1990b): 10-17.

Yu, K-J. *"The Study of the Systematic Methods of Landscape Aesthetics: Lake Landscape as an Example; The Thought of Planners Across Centuries,"* ed. S-X Bao. Chinese Architecture Project Press (1990c).

Yu, K-J. *"The Ecological Philosophy of Feng-shui Theory and the Ideal Landscape Patterns: The Research Report of Systematic Ecology."* The Laboratory of Systematic Ecology of the Chinese Academy of Sciences, no. 1 (1991): 6-15.

Yu, K-J. *"An Exploration of the Meaning of Natural Landscape Environment: The Rhythmic Beauty of the Typical Valley Landscape in South Taihang Mountain."* Beijing Forestry University Sinica 13, no. 1 (1991a): 9-17.

Yu, K-J. 1991b, *"Landscape Sensitivity and the Estimation of Threshold."* Geographic Research 10, no. 2 (1991b): 38-51.

Yu, K-J. 1991c, *"From the Selection of the Satisfactory Landscape to the Design of the Whole Ecological System of Mankind; The Theory, Method and Application of Landscape Ecology."* Chinese Forestry Publishing House, ed. D-N Xiao (1991c): 161-70.

Yu, K-J. 1991d, *"The Significance and Structure of the Spatial Beauty of Greenland,"* for the occasions of the 60th anniversary of the Chinese Academy of Horticulture and the corpus of thesis for the 6th annual conference of Gardening (ed. Chinese Academy of Horticulture), Wanguo Academic Publishing House (1991d): 21-23.

Yu, K-J. *"The Basin Experience and the Ecological Restraint Landscape of Chinese Cultivation Culture."* Beijing Forestry University Sinica 14, no. 4 (1992).

Yu, K-J. *"The Relationship of Garden Landscape Preference and Social Cultural Background."* Chinese Association of Science, thesis corpus of the 1st youth academic annual conference, Volume of Cross Sciences, (1992a): 169-75.

Yu, K-J. "*Landscape Dreams and Ecological Experience: Appreciating the Essence of Beauty of the Chinese Garden in the Ideal Landscape Pattern; The Noble Senses of the Garden*." Thesis corpus of 1st Chinese Seminar of Landscape and Garden Aesthetics, ed. J-L Li. Nanjing Publishing House (1994).

Yu, K-J and Q-P Ji. "*The Research and Solutions of the Aesthetic Differences in Landscape between Experts and Public*." *Chinese Garden* (1990): 219-23.

Zhang, D-N. *An Outline of the History of Chinese Philosophy*, Chinese Social Science Press, 1982.

The History of Chinese Civilization, Vol. 1, Hebei Education Publishing House.

Publishers of Architecture, Art, and Design
Gordon Goff: Publisher

www.oroeditions.com
info@oroeditions.com

Published by ORO Editions

10 9 8 7 6 5 4 3 2 1 First Edition

Library of Congress data available upon request. World Rights: Available

English Edition ISBN: 978-1-943532-75-9
Chinese Editions ISBN Copyright © 1998, The Commercial Press, Beijing, China

Color Separations and Printing: ORO Group Ltd.
Printed in China.

International Distribution: www.oroeditions.com/distribution

ORO Editions makes a continuous effort to minimize the overall carbon footprint of its publications. As part of this goal, ORO Editions, in association with Global ReLeaf, arranges to plant trees to replace those used in the manufacturing of the paper produced for its books. Global ReLeaf is an international campaign run by American Forests, one of the world's oldest nonprofit conservation organizations. Global ReLeaf is American Forests' education and action program that helps individuals, organizations, agencies, and corporations improve the local and global environment by planting and caring for trees.